The Spiritual Guide

Miguel de Molinos

Edited by Trevor Boiling

The Lutterworth Press

The Lutterworth Press
P.O. Box 60
Cambridge
CB1 2NT

www.lutterworth.com
publishing@lutterworth.com

First Published in 2006

ISBN (10): 0 7188 3054 7
ISBN (13): 978 0 7188 3054 0

British Library Cataloguing in Publication Data
A catalogue record is available from the British Library

Printed in the United Kingdom by
Athenaeum Press, Gateshead

Contents

For Sarah, Kevin
and Sofia

Introduction

(1)

In 1675 the Spanish priest Miguel de Molinos published at the age of forty-seven a concise and simple introduction to the art of interior prayer, or contemplation: the *Spiritual Guide*, "which disentangles the soul and leads it by the interior way to perfect contemplation and the rich treasure of interior peace."[1] On its first pages it carried the approbation of some of the most notable clerics of various orders, and was an immediate success, passing through several editions in the original Spanish, and being translated into Latin, French, Italian, and English.

For ten years the *Spiritual Guide* was immensely popular, and Molinos himself enjoyed huge popular veneration as a spiritual director and teacher. Twelve years' residence had made him a Roman citizen, and few would recall his arrival from Valencia at the age of thirty-five as a champion for the canonization of one Francisco Simón, whose case foundered. By this time Molinos had friends in high places, including Pope Innocent XI, who secured apartments for him in the papal palace. Spectacularly, however, ten years following publication of the *Spiritual Guide*, and after a protracted heresy trial, lasting two years, for his alleged illuminist views, he was found guilty on sixty-eight charges, and condemned to life in prison, where he died nine years later.

We do not have a great deal of information regarding Molinos' beliefs, apart from the *Spiritual Guide* itself, and a second hitherto unpublished book titled the *Defence of Contemplation*, his rebuttal of the charges of heresy. Additionally, there is the Bull *Coelestis Pastor*, which sets out the so-called sixty-eight heretical "propositions". There is also the Church's general condemnation of Quietism of which they believed Molinos to have been if not the originator, then a pivotal figure. And of course we have the continued popularity of the *Spiritual Guide* in Protestant circles, for it was here that translations into English, German and Dutch were frequently reprinted long after the text had disappeared from the Roman Catholic world.

There is very little that is exceptionable in the *Spiritual Guide*, for it is simply a short and very readable presentation of traditional mystical teaching, notably that of St Teresa of Ávila and her friend and colleague St

John of the Cross, both of whom wrote at the height of Spain's Golden Age, a century before Molinos. Like these two mystics he also wrote for beginners on the path of interior prayer, as well as describing the higher reaches of mystical contemplation. But what marked out Molinos above all was that he wrote for the ordinary layperson, not exclusively for those in the cloister.

The book begins by distinguishing in terms first set out by Richard of St Victor in the twelfth century the two types of prayer: discursive meditation and interior or silent contemplation. There are many, asserts Molinos, who live in spiritual aridity and discomfort, though ready to advance from discursive, or "active", prayer to a more advanced, "passive" contemplation. There are five signs, says Molinos, by which an experienced director would know when to encourage a person to make the transition from the active mode to the passive: 1) the first and most important, that they can no longer engage in discursive meditation or, if they can, find it upsetting and fatiguing; 2) that although they lack devotion, they seek solitude and avoid the company of others; 3) that they find devotional books disagreeable, for they tell them nothing of the interior peace they possess, though without knowing it; 4) that though they are unable to meditate they are still determined to persevere in prayer; 5) that they recognize higher knowledge and their own confusion, hate sin, and love God (Book 1, chapter 16).

The remedy for these disquieting signs, advises Molinos, is to seek out a competent spiritual director, or 'guru' – harder than it sounds, as St Teresa's biography tells us. She records instances of her own mishandling as a result of the ineptitude of many purporting to be experts, who clearly were not. However, Molinos and his colleagues set a good example, travelling throughout Italy, reviving the practice of contemplation in monasteries and convents, where it had fallen into disuse. Significantly, a body of twelve thousand letters from those spiritually troubled were found in Molinos' possession at the time of his trial.

That Molinos was very percipient in his advice to beginners in interior prayer is evidenced by many passages in the *Spiritual Guide*. His warning against straining in prayer, for instance, identifies a mistake made by beginners in all kinds of meditation, using "meditation" here in its contemporary sense. For instance, following is the sort of advice given by Dhiravamsa, a Buddhist living here in the West, regarding Vipassana meditation and "mindfulness," which has clear affinities with Molinos' "acquired contemplation" described in the first book of the *Spiritual Guide*:

> Watch any state of mind, whether it be worry, anxiety, wandering, thinking, talking – any condition of mind – watch carefully, closely, *without thinking about it*, without trying

to control it and without interpreting any thought; because this is very important when you come to the deeper level of meditation . . . In the deep state, all concepts and all names or words must be given up completely so that the mind can remain silently watchful and because of that, creative energy comes into being. . .You can sense creative energy in the state of passive watchfulness or in the state of stillness and complete tranquillity.[2]

The keyword to the *Spiritual Guide* is "two". There are *two* ways of approach to God, *two* sorts of prayer, *two* sorts of devotion, *two* sorts of darkness, *two* sorts of spiritual men, *two* kinds of silence, *two* kinds of penance, *two* sorts of contemplation. On the one hand Molinos accepts the normal "exterior" system taught and practised by the Church, which he gently puts aside, while on the other he puts forward his alternative "interior" system. To bring out the difference between the two ways – the exterior, active way, and the interior, passive way of Quiet – I summarize the distinctions as follows:

1. Approach God:
a. By rational thought, by meditation, which is remote – the way of beginners.
b. By contemplation, which is by pure faith: detached, pure and interior – the way of proficients.
2. Prayer:
a. Is tender and delightful, loving, and full of emotions: the prayer of beginners to *gain* the soul.
b. Is dark, dry, desolate – the prayer of proficients to *purify* the soul.
3. Devotion:
a. Is "accidental" and sense orientated, tempting to the instincts.
b. Devotion is "essential" and true, encouraging virtue.
4. Darkness and Aridity:
a. Unhappy, as it arises from wrongdoing, which deprives us of joy.
b. Or joyous, for it encourages virtue.
5. Spiritual persons:
a. Either outwardly oriented, given to reason and outward observance – the way of beginners, who strive towards a spiritual life, but achieve nothing.
b. Or "interior" persons, withdrawn in the presence of God, contemplating him in silence, and in whom he operates.
6. Solitude and Silence:
a. Either physical withdrawal from the world in search of peace.

b. Or devoted to "interior silence" – detached from all things: especially desire and one's own will – experience of the Void.
7. Penance:
a. Exterior, undertaken by oneself.
b. Interior, submitted to as God's will.
8. Contemplation:
a. Imperfect, active, acquired by our own efforts.
b. Perfect, infused and passive – truly to live in the Void (described in the third book).

Regrettably, Molinos found that many beginners would not persist long with the practice he taught, since they might well find it dull and apparently unrewarding. At such times he would insist (following St John of the Cross) that despite appearances to the contrary, God was *active* within them, in the darkness. Additionally, he urged people to learn to accept themselves, sin and all, advice that certainly antagonized the Jesuits who encouraged frequent confession, for essentially Molinos' spirituality called for inner penitence rather than outward austerities, as well as for frequent Communion.

His overall advice, then, was to avoid strain in meditation and contemplation, and neither should people force themselves to attend unrewarding Church services, or to read devotional books, or, when meditating, to struggle against disturbing and distracting thoughts. All of this, of course, was anathema to a more activist Jesuit spirituality, deriving as it did from the Ignatian "exercises," which were essentially "exterior", discursive, and imagistic.

Eventually the *Spiritual Guide* was perceived as a threat to the Jesuits' authority, for they placed strict emphasis on outward observance, and exercised much of their power through the confessional. Consequently they initiated an attack on Molinos and his particular brand of interior spirituality. Initially the attack failed, but eventually a far more serious attack was prepared – a prosecution before the court of the Holy Inquisition on 263 charges of heresy, which were then reduced to 68. The heresy of which Molinos was accused and finally convicted was that of "illuminism", or Quietism, of which more shortly.

Molinos' trial was long and squalid, and although at times accusations of heresy seemed unlikely to stick, new charges of sexual misconduct were levelled against him, charges that collapsed at the trial. Eventually he was convicted at the chapel of the Santa Maria Sopra Minerva convent, and on this final day – 21 December 1687 – the Minerva was so full that a crowd gathered in the street outside, made up of those unable to gain entrance. Members of the College of Cardinals, bishops, eminent clerics, the principal ambassadors, all filled the seats as Molinos, on his knees in the centre of the choir, holding a lighted candle in his manacled hands, read his abjuration and heard his sentence of life imprisonment.

A contemporary English chronicler, Bishop Burnet, wrote: "Molinos' bearing was not that of one oppressed by the weight of findings against him, nor of one who repents his actions or his heresy. Indeed the mildness of the censure laid upon him who was so little humble or repentant seemed rather due to an insufficiency of proof than to the clemency of the judges."[3] All present testified to his dignified bearing at the trial, and to his air of self-assured equanimity, a self-assured equanimity born out by the remarks made to his gaoler as he was led from the chapel: "We shall know on the Day of Judgement which of us is right, you or I,"[4] sentiments that are echoed in various pages of the *Spiritual Guide* and the *Defence of Contemplation*, as we see from these lines in the *Spiritual Guide*:

> If almighty God has worked so many miracles in the chaos of the Void, then what will he do for you who are made in his own image and likeness, if you persevere with courage, quiet and resigned, and with a true knowledge of your own nothingness? Happy indeed is the person who though troubled, afflicted and desolate, remains constant within. . . .

Could this be a self-portrait? Molinos died after nine years' imprisonment on 21 December 1696, the anniversary of his final appearance in the Minerva, at the age of sixty-eight.

(2)

A sense o'er all my soul impressed
That I am weak, yet not unblessed,
Since in me, round me everywhere,
Eternal strength and wisdom are. . . .

S. T. Coleridge

With Molinos the great tradition of Western mysticism, which had originated with the Victorines, flowered in Germany, England, the Netherlands and, finally, in Spain, came to an end. It is well known that few mystics had felt at ease within the confines of Church doctrine. Meister Eckhart, perhaps the greatest of them all, was fighting a prosecution for heresy when he died. So what is the crux of the quietist conundrum, a conundrum that was so troublesome to clerics and mystics alike, and which culminated in Molinos' condemnation, the final scene in the drama?

Essentially, the controversy hinges on what we make of Eckhart's notion of "detachment" (abgescheidenheit), which Molinos calls the Void (nada). Both these concepts denote an ego-less mode of being in which our normal ego-centredness is suspended to yield a sense of profound peace and well-being. As Eckhart would say, it indicates a sense of "non-being", which results from our taking up a position within the "Godhead" – the "God beyond Deity".

Similarly, Molinos talks of the state of union as a dwelling in the "Void", a state of consciousness also beyond the created ego. Thus the Void is that state experienced when the powers of the soul are gathered into its apex, the point at which it transcends all creatureliness. As such, it is a state of consciousness that undermines the whole principle of the ego, and all that flows from it. Paradoxically, then, it is a state of *nothingness* that is nevertheless a *plenitude*, an *emptiness* that is a *fullness*, a *passivity* that is an *activity*. It is what I refer to as the "dynamic passivity of the Void", which is the nature of ultimate reality, and in which we participate in the divine union.

The harmony of serenity and power that characterizes ultimate reality – the dynamic passivity of the Void – receives a plain statement in the work of Abhinavagupta, the eleventh-century Hindu exponent of Kashmir Shaivism. In his metaphysical system the masculine Shiva is envisaged in dynamic relation to the feminine Shakti, both of whom are conceived metaphorically as "the Heart":

> The Heart is the very Self of Shiva . . . and of the . . . Goddess who is inseparable from Shiva. Indeed the Heart is the site of their union, of their embrace. . .The Heart is the Ultimate which is both utterly transcendent to and yet totally immanent in all created things. It is the ultimate essence. . .The Heart is the fullness of the unboundedness of Shiva, the plenum of being that overflows continuously into manifestation. . .The Heart of Shiva is not a static or inert absolute, however. . . the non-dual Kashmir Shaiva tradition considers it to be in a state of perpetual movement, a state of vibration in which it is continuously contracting and expanding, opening and closing, trembling, quivering, throbbing, waving, and sparkling. The intensity and speed of this movement is such that paradoxically it is simultaneously a perfect dynamic stillness.[5]

Above all, however, consciousness of the Void is emphatically *not* a negation of the individual will – which is Quietism (or pantheism) – for it is an amalgam of the individual consciousness *and* the universal, of the active *and* the passive, in which the creature most certainly cooperates with the creator. Following is a brief collation of passages by Meister Eckhart that will serve to illustrate the sort of polarities of which I speak, the most important being the state of *nothingness* (the Void), which is also a *fullness*. Additionally, in these passages the role of the individual will is quite clearly discernible, thus giving the lie to the suggestion that Eckhart – or Molinos – advocated some kind of quietistic inertia. It is clear from what follows that when we set aside our own will, then God becomes active on our behalf:

> If therefore the heart is to be in a state of preparedness to receive the All Highest, then it must rest in nothingness, and that offers the greatest of all possibilities. Since the detached heart is at the highest point, then it must rest in nothingness, for that is where the greatest receptivity exists.
>
> When a person takes leave of their ego in obedience, and strips themselves, then God must needs enter into them, for when someone does not want anything for themselves, then God must will for them what he wills for himself.[6]
>
> If it is the case that a man is emptied of things, creatures, himself and God, and if still God could find a place in him to act, then we say: as long as that (place) exists, this man is not poor with the most intimate poverty. For God does not intend that man shall have a place reserved for him to work in, since the true poverty of spirit requires that man shall be emptied of God and all his works, so that if God wants to act in the soul, he must be the place in which he acts – and that he would like to do. For if God once found a person as poor as this, he would take the responsibility of his own action and would himself be the scene of action, for God is one who acts within himself. It is here, in this poverty, that man regains the eternal being that once he was, now is, and evermore shall be.[7]

(3)

> People do not need to think so much what they should do, but rather how they should be. If we are good, then our works are radiant. If we are just, then our works also are just. We should not think to found sanctity on doing things, but rather on a way of being, for works do not sanctify us, rather we sanctify works. . . .
>
> Meister Eckhart

The Buddhist philosopher Nishida Kitaro (1870-1945) was one of the leading thinkers of the Kyoto School of Buddhist philosophy. In an article in *Encyclopedia Britannica* we find a clear explanation of

Nishida's thought that endorses the position Eckhart and Molinos set out in relation to detachment, as well as his insistence on the utmost importance of the individual consciousness *within* the universal. It is quite apparent from what follows that what Nishida has in mind with his concept of "absolute nothingness" – in contradistinction to the quietist position – is to accord equal status to the universal *and* the individual, just as all orthodox Christian mystics do, Molinos included:

> The "Non-self" of Nishida is the ultimate reality where all subject-object cleavage is overcome. In accordance with Buddhist tradition he called it "Nothingness" and sought to derive the individual reality of everything in the world, whether it be a thing or a self, from the supreme identity of nothingness . . . the "Non-self" of Nishida establishes itself as true individuality in the absolute Nothingness, which includes, not excludes, the individual reality of the thing-in-itself (the ultimate reality of things). . .Nishida thus seeks to clarify the significance of the individual and the universal from the viewpoint of Absolute Nothingness. Thus he propounds that Nothingness. . . is the universal to be sought behind the universal concept and, at the same time, the abyss of Nothingness in which the self as the individual is crystallized.

Now the function of Buddhist yoga – just as it is of Molinos' prayer – is to still the discursive and discriminative functions of the mind to allow it to return to potentiality, so that the world may be perceived once more in all its "suchness", or "nothingness". In this state we are aware again of the joyous and spontaneous play of the Void. In the words of the Buddhist sage Te-Shan, "Only when you have no thing in your mind and no mind in things are you vacant and spiritual, empty and marvellous."[8] It is this same dynamic passivity of the Void that I have described here in relation to Buddhism that Molinos enjoyed, and which explains much of the meaning and value of his *Spiritual Guide.*

In fact, the compassion that the Zen Buddhists say is contingent upon emptiness (*ku soku jihi*) has its exact counterpart in what Molinos and Christian writers simply called "humility", as we see in these words from Meister Eckhart: "Detachment comes so close to nothingness that there is nothing that can stand between nothingness and it. Therefore, perfect detachment cannot exist without humility."

And from the *Spiritual Guide*:

> Those who have attained perfect interior humility don't get anxious about anything because they despise themselves for their failings, ingratitude, and wretchedness, all of which cause them a great

deal of heartache. This is the sign by which you know the sincerely humble of heart. But the happy beings who have such a holy hatred of their own ego live immersed in the depths of the Void from where God raises them up to infuse his divine wisdom, thereby filling them with light, peace, tranquillity, and love.

It should be clear now that authentic spirituality of all times and places has condemned quietistic modes of thought, preferring rather to give equal emphasis to the individual *and* the universal, the active *and* the passive. I conclude now by quoting firstly a description of the Taoist *wu-wei*, expressing so succinctly as it does the principle of "dynamic passivity". Finally, I give two brief excerpts from the *Spiritual Guide* itself, which in theological language typical of the West speaks of the same creative passivity denoted by *wu-wei*. First, here is J.C. Cooper describing the Taoist principle of *wu-wei* (dynamic passivity):

> It is the doctrine of inaction or non-action, but only a superficial outlook interprets it as laissez-faire, in the sense of indifference, for the Taoist is not indifferent. . . . If any translation should be attempted, possibly "non-interference," or "letting-go" is the best . . . . At the higher level it is the desirelessness, the dispassionateness which leads to the release from tensions. . . . Action is normally the outcome of the incessant, and usually feverish, working of the mind. . . .*wu-wei* is the "actionless activity". . . . *Wu-wei* is not the end of all action but the cessation of motivated action. . . . Actionlessness is an inward quality; it may be passive but it is a creative passivity.[9]

And now Miguel de Molinos:

> The means to arrive at this exalted state of renewal, and the most immediate way to be united to the Highest Good, to your primordial origin and supreme peace, is the Void. Endeavour always to be immersed in this Void of your nothingness, for it's God's way of working miracles in your soul. Clothe yourself in this Void and strive for it to be your constant support and dwelling place, until you lose yourself in it, and I assure you that if you're always in the Void, then God will be fully in your soul.
>
> Oh, how blessed are those who are dead and annihilated in this way! For now they live not for themselves, but God lives in them. And in all truth we can say that they're like the phoenix, because they're reborn, changed, spiritualized, transformed, and deified.

Notes

1. Although the *Spiritual Guide* was translated into English at the end of the seventeenth century, it was this truncated version that was reprinted in this country up to and including the twentieth century (reprinted in 1907 and 1911, edited by Kathleen Lyttelton, with an introduction by H. Scott Holland). The present version is the first full, modern translation and is based on the *princeps romana* published by Barral in Barcelona in 1974, edited with an introduction by the Spanish poet, José Ángel Valente. I am indebted to Paul Burns of Burns and Oates for his careful editing of my own translation. I am also indebted to the late J.M Cohen whose *Common Experience* (a) first stimulated my interest in Miguel de Molinos, and whose article "Some Reflections on the Life and Work of Miguel de Molinos" (b) was of help to me in this introduction.
a. J.M Cohen and J-F Phipps, *The Common Experience*, London, 1979.
b. *Studies in Mystical Literature*, Volume 1, Number 3, Spring 1981 (published by the English Department of Tunghai University, Taichung, Taiwan).
2. Dhiravamsa, in *Modern Mystics and Sages* by Anne Bancroft, London, 1978, pp. 146-7.
3. Dr. G Burnet, "A Letter Writ from Rome to One in Holland concerning the Quietists," written in the year 1687.
4. Ibid.
5. P.E. Muller, *The Triadic Heart of Shiva: Kaula Tantricism of Abhinavagupta in the Non-Dual Shaivism of Kashmir*, New York, 1989.
6. These extracts from Oliver Davies, *God Within*, London, 1988, pp. 59-65.
7. Meister Eckhart, in *Zen and the Birds of Appetite* by T. Merton, New York, 1968, p. 110.
8. Te-Shen in *The Way of Zen* by by Alan W. Watts, Harmondsworth, 1962, p. 151.
9. J. C. Cooper, *Yin and Yang: The Taoist Harmony of Opposites*, Wellingborough, 1982, p. 61.

The Spiritual Guide

Which disentangles the soul and leads it by the interior way to perfect contemplation and the rich treasure of interior peace

By Miguel de Molinos

To the Reader

There is nothing more difficult than to please everyone, or easier or more common than to criticize new publications. Every book that is published, without exception, is vulnerable on both counts, even though it enjoys every possible patronage. What will become of this little book without patronage, whose subject matter is mysticism and therefore hard to assimilate, and which is commonly subjected to criticism and acrimony? If you don't understand it, dear reader, don't criticize it on account of this.

Ordinary people will read and hear about these spiritual matters, but will not succeed in understanding them. If you condemn it, then you condemn yourself to the company of all those educated people to whom, as St Dionysius said, God doesn't communicate this wisdom as he does to the simple and uneducated, even though they're commonly held to be ignorant. Mystical knowledge is nothing to do with intelligence, but rather with experience: it's not created, but absorbed, not studied, but received, and so, therefore, it's very safe and effective, of great help, and enormous benefit.

Mystical knowledge is not acquired through hearing about it or by continually reading books but through the generous infusion of the divine spirit, whose grace is communicated with delightful intimacy to the simple and uneducated (Matt. 11).

There are some educated people who have never read about these matters and some spiritual people who so far haven't had any experience of them, and so for one reason or another they condemn them – the former out of ignorance, and the latter through lack of experience. It's a fact that anyone who has had no experience of this intimacy won't be able to pronounce on these mysterious secrets, but on the contrary will be appalled as many usually are when they hear

about the miracles God's love works in the soul and see no evidence
of this gentleness in themselves. Who will set a limit to God's
goodness? God doesn't call the strongest on merit, but the weakest
and most wretched, so that his infinite mercy may shine the more.

This knowledge is not theoretical, but practical, where experience
has an overwhelming advantage over the most informed and astute
speculation, and because those learned people who are purely
scholastic don't have the experience, they condemn it. For this reason
St Teresa advised her spiritual father to deal with spiritual matters
only with spiritual persons: "Because if they know only one way, or
they've stopped in the middle, they won't succeed."

It will be evident those who condemn the teaching in this book are not
experienced in this practical and mystical knowledge, and have not read
St Dionysius, St Augustine, St Gregory, St Bernard, St Thomas, St
Bonaventure, and many other saints and doctors approved by the Church,
who endorse, propound and teach as experts the doctrine of this book.

You should bear in mind that this teaching is not intended for
everyone, but only those whose senses and passions are well
disciplined, and who are already practised and proficient in prayer,
and called by God to the interior way. It is these people that this book
wishes to guide and encourage by removing for them the obstacles
that block the way to perfect contemplation.

I have tried to make the style of this book devout, uncluttered, and
beneficial, and without any display of eloquence or theological subtlety.
I have simply tried to teach the naked truth, humbly, simply and clearly.
It's not surprising that new books on spirituality are published every
day, because God always has new knowledge to impart and people
always have need of instruction. And not everything has been said or
written, and so there will always be a need to write until the end of
time. The light that God communicated to his Church through the
Angelic Doctor, St Thomas, was wholly laudable; but when he was
about to die, he himself said that God had communicated so much
light to him at that time that what he had written up till then was
worthless. And so God has – and always will have – new light to
communicate, without this infinite knowledge ever being exhausted.

The many and substantial problems on the interior way should not
deter you, because what is of great value obviously demands a lot.
Take heart, for not only will the people mentioned here succeed, but
so will many others through inner strength and with divine grace. It
was never my intention to deal with contemplation or to defend it, like
all those very erudite people who have published whole books full of
sound reasoning and teachings of the saints and holy scripture to

confute the opinion of those who have condemned contemplation and still do through not having experienced it or even understood it at the intellectual level. Long years of experience (with the many people who have relied on my inadequacy to show them the interior way to which they have been called) have taught me the great need there is to remove for them the obstacles, wilful inclinations, emotions and attachments that completely block their way and the road to perfect contemplation.

The whole of this practical book is directed to this primary objective, because it's not sufficient to assert the validity of the interior way of contemplation against those who contradict it, if you don't remove the obstacles that block the way to the spiritual ascent of those who are called and confident. To this end I have availed myself more of what God in his infinite goodness has inspired in me and taught me than the instruction I have derived from reading books.

Sometimes, though not often, I quote some practical and experienced authority, so that it will be apparent that the teaching in this book is not strange or unusual. This, then, has been my first objective – not to guarantee the interior way, but to remove obstacles from it. My second objective has been to instruct directors so that they don't hinder the way of those called by these hidden paths to interior peace and supreme happiness. May God grant in his infinite mercy that what is so earnestly desired has succeeded. I am aware that many, through inexperience, will criticize what is taught here, but I trust to God that some of those he has called to this knowledge will benefit, for if they do so I will consider my time well spent. This has been my only wish, and if God, who never changes, accepts and makes use of this sincere desire, I shall be content, even though harshly criticized.

Introduction

First Preface

On the two ways of approaching God: the first by meditation and discursive thinking; the second by pure faith and contemplation

(1) There are two ways to approach God, one by reasoning and discursive thinking, the other through pure faith, indistinct, general and intuitive awareness. The first is called meditation; the second interior recollection or acquired contemplation. The first is the way of beginners, the second of proficients. The first is based on information from the senses, the second is detached, pure and interior.

(2) When we are already accustomed to reflect on the mysteries with the help of the imagination and mental images, and to move from one object of attention to another, and from one thought to the next (though with little satisfaction from either), and thence to God himself, then God usually takes us by the hand if indeed he hasn't already called us and introduced us to the way of pure faith. If not, then God will cause us to disregard the intellect with all its thoughts and reflections, and to make progress by withdrawing us from our normal condition that is material and sense-orientated, to a state where by a simple and obscure awareness in faith we may aspire on the wings of love to our bridegroom, with no need now to love him on the prompting of the understanding, or information derived from it, for love arrived at in this way is short-lived and very dependent on external stimuli, which resemble drops of water that fall intermittently and spasmodically.

(3) The less we are dependent on external stimuli and the more we rely on God alone and his hidden teaching through the medium of pure faith, then the firmer, stronger and more durable our love will be. When we have acquired the knowledge that meditation and mental images can provide, if God then moves us on from this state by denying us the ability to think discursively, and leaves us in divine darkness to travel the straight road of pure faith, then we should let ourselves be led and not want to love meagerly and briefly, which is all that meditation allows.

We should accept that everything the world can offer, and the most sophisticated concepts of erudite men, are all useless. The beauty and goodness of our beloved infinitely surpass all our knowledge, showing us that the things of this world are truly inadequate to instruct us and to bring us to the true knowledge of God.

(4) We should grow in God's love, then, leaving all thought behind. Let us love God as God is in himself, and not as we picture God to be. And if he can't know God as God is in himself, let us love God without knowing him under the veil of obscure faith, just like a child who has never seen its father but completely believes what has been said about him and loves him as if it had in fact seen him.

(5) Those deprived of discursive thinking should not strain themselves or strive for clearer and more distinct knowledge. On the contrary, they should remain quiet, firm and steadfast, without the support of information from the senses. In this way they are poor in spirit and free from the demands of their natural appetites, thus allowing God to work within them, although they may seem to be alone, dry as they are and enveloped in darkness. All this might appear to them as idleness but is so only in relation to the activity of their senses, and not as regards God, who actively imparts true knowledge to them. In brief, the higher the spirit ascends, the more it becomes detached from the senses. Many people have arrived at this door, and still do, but there are few who have moved on, and still don't, because they lack an experienced guide. And those who have one, and have had one in the past, still fail because they don't totally submit to him.

(6) It may be objected that the will cannot love if the understanding cannot form clear and distinct ideas, for it's an accepted principle that one can love only what one knows. To this I would say that although the understanding does not operate by making distinctions, that is, by thinking discursively and employing images and concepts, nevertheless, it is aware and understands through dark, general and intuitive faith – an understanding that, although dark, indistinct and general, because it's supernatural, is actually a clearer and more perfect cognition of God that can be arrived at in this life, for all mental images based on sense data are immeasurably remote from God.

(7) We think more highly of God knowing that he is beyond our comprehension and that he transcends all understanding, than we do by conceiving him according to some image or thing of beauty, which is to understand him in our own crude manner (Mystical Theology 1,2). And so greater love and esteem for God flow from this indistinct, obscure and negative method of cognition than any other method that

is precise and based on the senses, as the former is more proximate
to God and abstracted from all particularities. The more this knowledge
depends on the created world, the further removed from God it is.

Second Preface
In what way meditation is different to contemplation

(8) St John Damascene, together with other saints, says that prayer
is "an ascent or elevation of the mind to God." God is above all his
creatures and you can't see God or communicate with him unless you
transcend all of them. This loving colloquy that the soul enjoys with
God, which is prayer, is divided into meditation and contemplation.

(9) When the mind ponders the mysteries of our holy faith in order
to comprehend its truths, by analyzing particular details and assessing
the circumstances to move the affections of the will, then this mental
reasoning with its pious affection is more properly called meditation.

(10) When you already understand these truths – whether through
the habit you acquired by reasoning or because God has given you
particular light – and you're fully aware of them, gazing upon them simply,
quietly, calmly and silently, with no further need for thought or reasoning
or any other proof to convince you, and when your will loves these truths,
wondering at them and delighting in them, then strictly speaking this is
called the prayer of faith, or of quiet, interior recollection or contemplation.

(11) This is what St Thomas, with all the other mystical teachers,
calls "a simple, gentle and quiet gaze on the eternal truth, without
reasoning or reflection." But if you ponder and delight in God's presence
in his creation, and especially in Christ's humanity as the most perfect
of this creation, then this is not true contemplation, as St Thomas says.
The reason for this is that the above are all means to know God as he
is in himself, and although Christ's humanity is the most holy and perfect
means to approach God and the chief instrument of our salvation and
the channel through which we receive every blessing we could hope
for, nevertheless, the humanity is not the Highest Good, which rather
consists in seeing God. But as Christ is who he is more through his
divine nature than his humanity (because his divinity is inseparable from
his humanity) then those who think of God and continually gaze upon
him by the same token always think of Christ and contemplate him.
This is especially true of contemplatives, whose faith is more sincere,
pure and practised.

(12) Whenever the end is reached, then the means cease, and when

the ship arrives in the harbour, then the voyage is over. And so those who have tired themselves with meditation and have attained to the quiet, calm tranquillity of contemplation, must then curtail their thinking and rest quietly with a loving attention and gaze on God. In this way we contemplate and love God, and gently set aside all those images that come to us, thus pacifying our understanding in the presence of God. And so our memory will be recollected and fixed entirely on God, content with a general and intuitive awareness of him in faith, with our will completely devoted to loving him, thereby deriving the maximum spiritual nourishment.

(13) St Dionysius says: "As for you, dear Timothy, in your mystical contemplation forsake the senses and the workings of the intellect; reject all intelligible things deriving from the senses as well as all else that is, and is not, so that in an inexpressible way you may raise yourself to God who transcends all knowledge and creation."

(14) And so it is necessary to reject all created things, and everything that comes to us through the senses that is intelligible and belongs to the emotions – in short, everything that is, and is not – and surrender ourselves entirely to God who will restore to us everything we have given up, and in addition give us the strength and power to love him more ardently, a love that will sustain us in this holy and blissful silence, which is worth more than all the activities of the mind put together.

St Thomas says: "What the understanding can know about God in this life is very little, but what the will can love counts for a great deal."

(15) When you attain this state you must withdraw totally within yourself, to your innermost centre, where you will find God's image. In this way you will practise loving attention to God, in silence and obliviousness of all things; you will exercise the will in perfect resignation, listening to God and communing with him alone, as if there were just the two of you in the whole world.

(16) With good reason the saints say that in meditation you're actively engaged to your advantage, whereas in contemplation you're passive, calm, peaceful and enraptured, and to far greater advantage. Meditation sows and contemplation reaps; meditation seeks and contemplation finds; meditation chews the food, contemplation savours it and is nourished by it.

(17) All this was said by the mystic Bernard in commenting on the words of Our Lord: "Seek and you shall find, knock and it shall be opened to you. Reading offers solid food to the mouth, meditation chews it, prayer brings out the flavour, and contemplation is the true sweetness that gladdens and refreshes the heart." All of the above explains meditation and contemplation and the difference between them.

Third Preface
An explanation of the difference between acquired and active contemplation and infused and passive contemplation, and the signs by which you will know when God wishes you to move on from meditation to contemplation

18) There are also two ways of contemplation, one imperfect, active and acquired, the other infused and passive. The active way (which we have been speaking about until now) is the one we can attain by our own efforts, assisted by divine grace. It consists in withdrawing the faculties and senses and in preparing ourselves for whatever God sends us.

(19) St Bernard recommends this active contemplation when he comments on the words "I will hearken what the Lord God will say concerning me" (Ps.84:8). v.8). He comments as follows: "Mary chose the better part; although perhaps the humble lot of Martha is of no less merit in the sight of God, yet Mary's choice is praised. Thus the lot of Mary is certainly to be chosen (for our part), but if the lot of Mary is to be visited upon us, it is to be borne with patience."

(20) St Thomas also recommends this acquired contemplation, with the following words: "The more closely a person unites his soul or that of another to God, so much the more acceptable is the sacrifice to God; and therefore it is more acceptable to God that a person apply his soul and that of others to contemplation than to action." This is a very clear statement to silence those critics who condemn acquired contemplation.

(21) The more closely we approach God, or endeavour to ensure that we and others may attain God, then the more acceptable this is to God. St Thomas concludes from this that contemplation rather than activity is more pleasing and acceptable to God. And neither can it be said that the saint is talking here of infused contemplation, because it's not in our power to apply ourselves to infused contemplation, but only to acquired.

(22) Although it's said that with God's help we can apply ourselves to acquired contemplation, nevertheless, we should not take it upon ourselves to move from the state of meditation to acquired contemplation without the advice of an experienced director who will know for sure if we're called to this interior way by God. But if a director is not available, we might know the right time through a book

that deals with these matters that has been sent by divine providence to show what has been happening in our interior life without our being aware of it. But even though we might be encouraged by information from a book to leave meditation for the quiet of contemplation, we shall always have an earnest wish for better instruction.

(23) And so that you may be better informed on this point, I want to give the signs by which to recognize this vocation to contemplation. The first and most important sign is the inability to meditate, and if a person does meditate it will be with obvious anxiety and fatigue, providing this condition doesn't arise from some physical indisposition, some natural disinclination, from a mood of depression, or dryness due to lack of preparation.

(24) You will know that it's none of these problems, but rather a genuine calling, when you spend a day, a month, or many months unable to think discursively in prayer. St Teresa puts it this way: "God guides us to contemplation, and then our mind becomes very inhibited in meditating on the Passion of Christ, because meditation is all to do with seeking God, and when we find God and are accustomed to seek him again by the operation of the will, we're not inclined to tire ourselves by further reasoning."

(25) The second sign is that although we're unable to find satisfaction in devotion based on the senses, we seek solitude and avoid conversation. The third sign is that the reading of books on spirituality becomes tedious to us because they don't address themselves to the interior gentleness we now experience, although we may not realize this. The fourth sign is that although we can no longer reason, nevertheless we're very determined to persevere in prayer. And the fifth sign is that we shall now have acquired a deeper understanding of ourselves together with great uncertainty about our own worth so that we then detest our shortcomings and have a higher regard for God.

(26) The other contemplation is perfect and infused, and is described in the following way by St Teresa: "God speaks to us and suspends our understanding, interrupting our thoughts and robbing us of the power of speech so that although we want to speak, we can't, except with great difficulty. We're aware that the heavenly teacher, without recourse to words, is instructing us by suspending our faculties, for if we use them we would do ourselves more harm than good. We're now in a state of bliss without knowing why. We burn with love with no idea how we love and although we delight in what we love we don't know the origin of this joy. We understand well enough that this bliss is not what the mind can come to desire. Yet the will embraces

this delight, without knowing how. And although we're incapable of understanding anything, yet we perceive that this bliss cannot be earned by any kind of effort whatsoever. It is a gift of the Lord of heaven and earth, who in short gives by his own power, to whom he pleases, and as he pleases. It is God alone who does it all, for his activity transcends our own nature" (Road to Perfection, ch. 25). It follows from these words of St Teresa that this perfect contemplation is infused, and that God gives it freely to whomever he pleases.

Fourth Preface
The main concern of this book is to encourage you to root out self-will to attain interior peace

(27) The way to interior peace consists in adapting ourselves in all things to God's will: "In all things we should submit our will to the divine will, for this is the peace of our will, that it be conformed in all things to the divine will" (Hugo Cardinalis, Psalm 13). Those who want everything their own way are oblivious of this ("The way of peace they have not known": Psalm 13), and neither do they want to travel this way, and so they lead bitter and empty lives, forever anxious and upset, for they fail to find the road to peace, which consists of total conformity to God's will.

(28) This conformity is the gentle yoke that leads us to the realm of interior peace and interior serenity. You will deduce from this that the rebellion of our own will is the principal cause of our anxiety and because we don't submit to the divine will we suffer so much distress and unease. Oh blessed souls! If we could only surrender ourselves to God's will in everything he ordains, what tranquillity we would enjoy, what peace and interior serenity we would feel, what supreme happiness and intimations of bliss we would experience! This, then, is to be the main concern of this book. May God grant me his divine light to reveal the hidden paths of this interior way and the supreme happiness of perfect peace.

First Book
On darkness, aridities and temptations with which God purifies souls, and on interior recollection or acquired contemplation

Chapter 1

For God to rest in your soul, you must constantly quieten your heart in any anxiety, provocation and distress

(1) You must realize that your soul is the centre, dwelling place and kingdom of God. But for that mighty king to rest on this throne of your soul, you must endeavour to keep it unblemished, quiet, empty and calm. It must be unblemished by faults and failings, quiet in anxiety, empty of emotions, desires and thoughts, and calm in provocation and distress.

(2) Always stay calm, then, to keep pure that living temple of God, and single-mindedly work, pray, obey and endure, without being disturbed in any way by whatever God may send you. For it's certain that for your own good and spiritual advantage, God will permit the jealous enemy to disturb this city of quiet and throne of peace with temptations, inappropriate thoughts and worries, and, in your day-to-day life, allow tiresome irritations and problems to upset you.

(3) Keep your heart calm and constant in any anxiety that these problems may bring you. Enter within yourself to overcome them, for you will find there the divine fortress that will defend you, protect you and fight for you. If you have a secure fortress you don't become anxious even though you're harassed by your enemies for when you enter within yourself they're mocked and defeated. The strong castle to overcome your enemies, both visible and invisible, with all their deceits and annoyances, is within yourself, for there dwells the divine help and supreme assistance; enter within yourself and all will be quiet, secure, calm and serene.

(4) Your main effort and concern must be to pacify this throne of your heart, in order that the supreme king may rest in it, and the way to stay calm is to enter within yourself by means of interior recollection. Interior prayer and loving recollection in the presence of God are your complete protection. When you feel yourself most threatened, withdraw to this region of peace where you will find the fortress. When you're most anxious, retreat to this refuge of prayer, the only weapon you have to overcome the enemy and quell anxiety. You mustn't abandon it while the storm lasts until you experience, like another Noah, tranquillity, security and serenity, and until you're resigned, devout, calm and encouraged.

(5) Finally, don't worry or lose faith when you're anxious: calm yourself once more whenever you become agitated, for all our heavenly father requires of you is that he may rest in your soul and find within you a rich treasure of peace. You must seek within yourself, by means of interior prayer, and with his divine grace, silence in turmoil, solitude in the crowd, light in darkness, indifference in abuse, courage in faintheartedness, strength in fear, resistance in provocation, peace in war, and calm in anxiety.

Chapter 2

Although you can't think discursively in prayer, you must persevere and not become anxious, because this is the way to your greatest happiness

(6) Like all those whom God calls to the interior way, you will be full of confusion and doubts when you can't reason in prayer. It will seem to you that God isn't helping you now as he used to, that this method of prayer isn't for you, that you're wasting your time when you find that you can't have a single thought as you once did.

(7) What confusion and distress this inability to reason will cause you! And if at this time you have no spiritual father experienced in the mystical way, unease will increase in you and confusion in him. Such a spiritual father will think that you're not sufficiently well prepared, and that for the safety of your conscience you need a general confession, and the result of your efforts will be the confusion of you both. Indeed, many are called to the interior way only to find that these spiritual fathers, instead of guiding them and helping them – because they don't understand what they're doing – succeed only in blocking their progress and disorientating them!

(8) Rest assured, then, that you mustn't turn back when you can't think discursively in prayer as this is your greatest happiness and an obvious sign that God wants you to journey in faith and silence with him, and to follow a path that's most advantageous and easiest for you. With a simple gaze, and loving attention to God, then, you're like a humble beggar before God, or like an innocent child who sinks onto the soft, safe breast of its beloved mother.

(9) This prayer is not only the easiest, it's the safest, because it's free from the workings of the imagination, which is always prey to the deceits of the devil and to the vagaries of melancholy mood. Moreover, discursive thought easily distracts you, and speculation can lead to the entanglements of self-absorption.

(10) When God wanted to teach his leader Moses and to give him the tablets of stone inscribed with the divine law, God called him to the mountain, when in his presence it grew dark, enveloped in gloom and dense cloud,

and Moses stood quiet without awareness and unable to think. After seven days God commanded him to go to the top of the mountain, where he revealed himself to him in all his glory and gave him complete comfort.

(11) In the same way, when God by extraordinary means wishes to acquaint you with the interior life, he requires you to travel in darkness and dryness to draw you to him, for he knows very well that to draw near to him and to understand what he has to teach you, the way forward isn't by means of your own effort and reasoning, but by resignation in silence.

(12) What a great example the patriarch Noah gave us! When everyone took him for a fool, and while adrift in a raging sea, with the whole world flooded and without sails or oars, and surrounded by wild animals inside an enclosed ark, he journeyed only with faith, without knowing or understanding what God had in mind for him.

(13) Of most importance to you – oh redeemed soul! – is patience, and not to abandon your prayer, even though you can't reason. Journey with firm faith and with sincere silence, dying to yourself with all your natural faculties; for God is who he is, and he doesn't change, and neither can God err, nor wish for anything other than your own good. Obviously those who must die to themselves must necessarily regret it; but how well the annihilated soul employs its time, silent and resigned in God, receiving God's divine guidance unhindered!

(14) The senses are incapable of receiving God's blessings. And so, if you wish to be happy and wise, be silent and believe, suffer and have patience, have confidence, and press on. For it's more important for you to be silent and let yourself be led by God, than to value the goods of this world. And although it might seem to you that you're doing nothing and are idle while silent, the advantages are infinite.

(15) Look at the little blindfolded donkey going round the wheel of the mill; for although he doesn't see or know what he's doing, he's very effective in grinding the corn, and although he doesn't like it, his master receives the benefit and the satisfaction. Most people think that the seed that lies in the earth for a long time will die. And then it pushes up, grows, and multiplies. God does the same thing for you when he deprives you of discursive thought; for thinking that you're doing nothing and that you have lost your way, in the course of time you will prosper and become detached and perfected, without ever having anticipated such good fortune.

(16) Try, then, not to become anxious, or turn back, even though you can't reason in prayer; suffer, be silent, remain in God's presence and persevere with firmness and trust in God's infinite goodness, for he will give you the steadfastness of faith, true light and divine grace. Press on in darkness, blindfolded, without thinking or reasoning; place yourself in God's loving fatherly hands, wishing only to do his divine will.

Chapter 3

Continuation

(17) Most saints and experts on mysticism think that you can't attain perfection and union with God through meditation and discursive thought alone, as these are only useful when commencing the spiritual way and until such time as you acquire the habit of self-knowledge, together with an awareness of the beauty of virtue and the ugliness of vice. This habit, according to St Teresa, can be acquired in six months, and according to St Bonaventure, in two.

(18) The many people who engage all their lives solely in meditation are surely to be pitied when they force themselves to reason even though God deprives them of discursive thought in order to carry them on to another state and more perfect prayer. And so for a very long time they remain imperfect and beginners, having made no progress nor even taken one step on the spiritual way. They rack their brains with the reading of detailed points, speculative thought, and tortuous reasoning, constantly seeking God on the outside when he is within themselves.

(21) Obviously Christ wanted us always to be perfect, especially the simple and uneducated. He demonstrated this very clearly when he chose his apostles among the most ignorant and humble, telling his eternal Father: "I thank you, Father, Lord of heaven and earth, for hiding these things from the learned and wise, and revealing them to the simple" (Matt. 11:25). And it's clear, too, that such people can't improve themselves by searching meditations and subtle reasoning, and yet they're as capable as the most learned of self-improvement through the affection of the will, in which it mainly consists.

(22) St Bonaventure teaches us not to think of anything, nor even of God, because it's an imperfection to form images and ideas in our mind however ingenious they may be, whether they concern the will, goodness, the Trinity or Unity, or the divine essence itself, as all these images and ideas, even though they may appear god-like, are not in themselves God, who allows no images of himself or any representation whatsoever.

(23) You will only unsettle yourself and even wish to abandon your prayer when you can't, or don't know how to, think discursively, although you may want to use your mind and are determined to do so. If God gives water from the dew to the raven's chicks abandoned by their parents who think they're worthless without black feathers, then God will surely help you, even though you can't speak or think, so long as you're trusting, and open yourself to heaven showing your need. Isn't it obvious that God will provide you with the nourishment you require?

(24) Clearly it's very distressing – and no small gift from God – for you to be deprived of the pleasures of the senses to which you're accustomed, and to journey only with holy faith along the dark deserted road to perfection. However, it has to be said that you can attain it only by this safe but difficult route. And so try to be firm and not turn back, even though you can't reason in prayer. Believe with courage, be quietly silent and persevere with patience, if you wish to be happy and attain divine union, consummate quiet and supreme interior peace.

Chapter 4

You mustn't become anxious or abandon your prayer when surrounded by aridities

(25) There are two kinds of prayer: the one, tender, pleasant, loving and full of feeling and emotion; the other, obscure, arid, full of temptation and darkness. The first is for beginners; the second for proficients and those on the way to perfection. God gives the first to win us over; the second to purify us. With the first he treats us like children and weaklings; with the second God begins to treat us like grown men.

(26) The first way is like the life of an animal and is typical of those who seek prayer that's pleasing to the senses, which is what God usually allows beginners, so that attracted by that tempting taste, like an animal drawn by an object that appeals to its senses, they commit themselves to the spiritual life. The second is appropriate to human life, and is characteristic of those who don't seek delight in the senses, but who struggle and fight against their own passions to overcome them and attain perfection, which is an undertaking proper to us.

(27) Rest assured that aridities are the means to your interior serenity, for they denote the absence of self-gratification, a shortcoming that arrests the progress of most spiritual persons, and even makes them turn back and give up prayer, as many do who persevere only while they enjoy the support of the senses.

(28) God uses aridities so that we don't realize the work he's doing within us, and in this way we're humbled; for if we were aware of what God is doing within us, self-satisfaction and complacency would take us over, and we would imagine we were doing something, and think we were very close to God, which would lead to our downfall.

(29) Acknowledge in your heart of hearts that in the first place you must give up all attachment to the senses to travel the interior way, and the means God uses to attain this end is through aridities, by depriving you of reflection and reasoning, which are a hindrance to your progress and an impediment to God's communication and work in you.

(30) You mustn't become anxious, then, or think that you're getting

nowhere, if you don't experience many feelings and emotions when you leave communion or prayer, because it's an obvious mistake. The farmer sows at one time and reaps at another. And so God, on occasions, and in his own time, will help you to resist temptation, and will give you, when you least expect it, sincere intentions and a stronger desire to serve him. And so that you don't allow yourself to be led astray by the insistent promptings of the jealous enemy who, to get you to abandon your prayer, will persuade you that you're doing nothing, and that you're wasting your time, I would like to make clear to you some of the great advantages to be gained from these aridities.

(31) The first thing is to persevere in prayer, from whose advantages come many others.

Second, you will experience world-weariness, a weariness that will gradually replace the inappropriate desires of your past life by producing other new ones to serve God.

Third, you will notice many faults in yourself that you hadn't noticed before.

In the fourth place, your conscience will prick you when you're going to do something wrong. At other times you will refrain from speaking, or from complaining, or retaliating; at still other times you will deny yourself some small pleasure, or you will avoid this or that occasion or conversation which formerly you would be very happy to indulge in without it bothering you.

Fifth, having made some slight mistake through weakness, your conscience will trouble you greatly.

Sixth, you will want to suffer to do God's will.

Seventh, you will be more inclined to virtue and find it easier to control yourself and overcome the strength of your passions and the enemies that hinder your progress.

Eighth, you will acquire a deep self-knowledge and even a disdain for yourself, and a reverence for God above all created beings, together with a disdain for the things of this world and a firm resolution not to give up prayer, even though you know it will be extremely tedious to you.

Ninth, you will experience greater interior peace, a desire to be modest and unassuming, and detachment from the things of the senses.

Finally, all those wrongs you will have stopped doing since you started your prayer will be due entirely to God working within you without your realizing it, by means of dry prayer, even though you're not aware of it while you're doing it, except in God's time and when he sees fit.

(32) All these advantages and many others are like new shoots born of the prayer you would like to abandon because it seems arid to you and whose fruit and nourishment you can't appreciate. Calm yourself and persevere with patience, for although you don't realize it, you're the one who is benefiting.

Chapter 5

Continuation, describing the various types of prayer; how you should ignore prayer that derives from the senses; and that although you don't think discursively, you're not idle

(33) There are two sorts of prayer, then: one is fundamental and direct, the other incidental and derived from the senses. Prayer that's fundamental involves an enthusiastic willingness to do good, to fulfil God's commandments, and to do all things in his service, even though out of weakness we don't carry them out as God would wish. This is true devotion, although you don't experience pleasure, tenderness or tears, but are on the contrary beset by temptations, aridities and darkness.

(34) Incidental and sense-orientated prayer arises when worthy intentions are joined to tenderness of the heart, gentleness, tears, or other emotions. You shouldn't indulge in this sort of prayer but rather disregard it and stay detached, for besides being generally dangerous, it's an enormous obstacle to your progress and to any advance on the interior way. And so you must practise only direct and fundamental prayer which is always in your power to attain, and if you try your best you will achieve it, assisted by divine grace. Moreover, it can be achieved through God, Christ, the mysteries, the Virgin, or the saints.

(35) Some people think that when they experience pleasurable prayer it's a favour from God and that they possess him for themselves, and then they yearn for this favour all their lives. But they're mistaken in this, for it is only nature's way of consoling us, or else it's a self-conscious absorption, which blocks all progress and prevents us from seeing the light, or from taking a single step on the road to perfection. The soul is pure spirit and has no emotions. Similarly, your interior life pertains to the will, and it, too, is spiritual, and has nothing to do with the senses. And so the soul is unaware whether or not it loves, and for the most part is unaware of its own activity.

(36) You will gather from all this that devotion pleasing to the senses is neither God nor spirit, but rather nature's snare, and so you must ignore

it, and persevere firmly in true prayer, guided by God, who will be your
light in darkness and aridity.

(37) Don't think that while you're dry and in darkness in God's
presence with silence and faith that you're doing nothing, that you're
wasting your time and being idle, for this idleness, according to St Bernard,
is the highest form of activity in God.

(38) Neither can you say that you're really idle, because although
you're not actively involved in this process, the Holy Spirit is working
within you. Besides, your soul is not completely inactive because it operates
spiritually: that is to say, simply and intimately. To be attentive to God,
draw near to him, follow his interior inspiration, receive his divine influence,
worship him in his most intimate centre, venerate him sincerely and
affectionately, ignore the many and bizarre impressions that arise in
prayer, and gently subdue and ignore temptation. These are all part of
this process, even though the effects of the Spirit are almost imperceptible,
because of the great tranquillity with which the Spirit produces such effects.

Chapter 6

You mustn't grow anxious when you're in darkness because this is the means to your greatest happiness

(39) There are two kinds of darkness, one unhappy, the other happy. The first is born of wickedness, and is unhappy, because it leads us to the eternal abyss. The second is the one God allows to establish you in virtue, and is happy because it strengthens and enlightens you. And so you mustn't become distressed or disconsolate when you're in obscurity and darkness, thinking that God, or the light you experienced previously, has deserted you. Rather, you must confidently continue with your prayer, for it's a clear indication that God in his compassion wishes to lead you to the interior way and the joyful road to Paradise. You will be very happy if you continue in this darkness, peaceful and resigned, to attain perfect quiet, true light, and your complete spiritual well-being.

(40) You must realize, then, that darkness is the way of those proficient in the spiritual life and that in it God establishes his throne. The supernatural light that God infuses in you will increase in this darkness and from it wisdom and sincere love are born, self-will is annihilated, and the conceptual thinking that obstructs the direct view of the divine truth is consumed. In this manner God leads you by the interior way to the prayer of quiet and perfect contemplation, which is experienced by so few. In this darkness, finally, God will purify those of your senses and emotions that obstruct the mystical way.

(41) Don't you think, then, that this darkness should be held in high regard? In darkness you must believe you're in God's presence and be gently and quietly attentive. You must wish to know nothing, nor seek favours, tenderness or devotion based on the senses, nor wish for anything other than God's will, as otherwise you won't do anything else in life but go round in circles, nor take one step towards perfection.

Chapter 7

In order to attain supreme interior peace God must discipline you in his own way, as the exercises and disciplines you take upon yourself are insufficient

(42) When you resolve firmly to discipline your senses to journey to the high mountain of perfection and union with God, his majesty will take you by the hand and dissuade you of your bad intentions, disordered appetites, complacency and self-love, and other hidden faults you're unaware of and which affect you deeply and prevent union with God.

(43) You will never attain this happiness however hard you try with exterior attempts at self-discipline until God disciplines you in his own way, because only he knows how to rid you of your hidden failings. If you persevere confidently, not only will he relieve you of your attachment to the things of this world but he will also check your tendency to indulge in the peripheral and supernatural effects of prayer, such as interior communications, raptures and ecstasies, and other manifestations of the Spirit that you think may provide you with support.

(44) God will do all this for you by means of the Cross and aridities if you freely commit yourself to him as you travel this dark, deserted road. You must do nothing of your own volition. Your only response is simply to suffer and be silent, quietly accepting everything God sends to discipline you: that is to say, bear your distress with equanimity, and don't place importance on exercises and disciplines you apply to yourself.

(45) The farmer thinks more of the plants he sows in the ground than those that spring up by themselves, because they never reach maturity. Similarly, God thinks more of the virtue he sows and instils in you when you're calm and serene in the Void, in your innermost centre, than all the other virtues you claim to acquire by yourself.

(46) What matters is to think of yourself as a blank piece of paper which God can write on as he pleases. What a great achievement it will be for you to be in prayer hours at a time, silent, resigned and humble, without doing anything, without knowing anything, nor wanting to understand anything.

Chapter 8

Continuation

(47) You will apply yourself to your prayer with renewed effort, but in a different way than hitherto, consenting to the secret and divine influences and allowing yourself to be formed and disciplined by God, which is the only way to overcome your ignorance and depravity. But to achieve this you must immerse yourself in the bitter sea of stress and suffering that will pierce you body and soul.

(48) You will also find that you're denied the support of the senses and even of those consolations you depended on most to help you in your distress. The well-springs of your faculties will dry up, and you won't be able to think or even have good thoughts about God. The sky will look like bronze to you and no light will come from it. Neither will you be consoled by the thought of former times when you were showered with so much light and devout encouragement.

(49) Your invisible enemies will pursue you with doubts, lustful suggestions and unclean thoughts, with inducements to impatience, arrogance, anger, cursing, and blasphemy of God's name, his sacraments and holy mysteries. You will experience lack of enthusiasm, weariness and repugnance for the things of God; obscurity and darkness of the understanding; faintheartedness, confusion and narrowness of spirit; lack of warmth and weakness of the will to resist, so that a small piece of straw will seem like a beam to you. Your helplessness will be so profound that it will seem to you that there's no longer a God for you and that you're incapable of having decent feelings. You will feel as if you're between two walls, in constant anxiety, with no hope of escaping such dreadful oppression.

(50) But don't be alarmed: all this is necessary to discipline you and to make you realize your own nothingness, and for the annihilation of all the passions and disordered appetites in which you normally delight. Finally, until God disciplines and forms you in his own way with this interior anguish, you won't cast the Jonah of the senses into the sea, however hard you try with your exercises and self-discipline, for you will remain at the beginning and you won't achieve loving quiet and supreme interior peace.

Chapter 9

You must not grow anxious or turn back on the spiritual way when you're threatened by temptations

(51) Your own nature is so despicable, arrogant and ambitious, so governed by its appetites, judgments and opinions that if temptation didn't curb it you would be hopelessly lost. And so God, moved to compassion by your abjectness and perversity allows various thoughts against the faith, horrible temptations, and insistent and distressing thoughts of impatience, arrogance, greed, lust, anger, blasphemy, cursing, feelings of desperation, and many other temptations, to encourage you in self-knowledge and humility. God humbles you in this way, thereby giving you a most effective medicine.

(52) "All our deeds," according to Isaiah (64:6) "are like stained garments," stained by vanity, complacency and self-love. They must be purified in the fire of anguish and temptation to be clean, perfect and acceptable in the sight of God.

(53) For this reason God disciplines you with the rough file of temptation when he calls you to him and wants you for himself. With this file he wears away the dross of arrogance, avarice, vanity, ambition, pretentiousness and self-love. And with it he humbles you, pacifies and purifies you, and makes you aware of your own nothingness. And with it also he purifies your heart so that everything you do will be of inestimable value.

(54) Many people become worried and anxious when they suffer this painful distress and think they've already begun to suffer eternal punishment in this life. And if through ill-luck they go to an inexperienced confessor they will fail to find reassurance and feel confused and frustrated.

(55) To gain interior peace you must understand that it's God in his kindness who humbles and disciplines you, for it's only in this way that you acquire self-knowledge and accept that you're the most despicable of people. How happy you will be if you remain quiet and

accept, too, that all these temptations are the work of the devil and prescribed by God for your own good and spiritual advantage.

(56) But you will say that it's not the work of the devil when people upset you but that it's their fault and their spite for having hurt and insulted you. In fact, this is simply one more sly and subtle temptation, because although God doesn't will others to abuse you, he does allow its effect on you and your effort to come to terms with it, so that you will appreciate the benefit of patience.

(57) If someone hurts your feelings, there are two things to consider: the malice of the person who hurts you, and the pain that you suffer. The malice is against God's will; the pain is in conformity with his will and allowed for your benefit, and so you must accept it as given by God. The Passion and death of Jesus were the result of Pilate's wickedness, and God certainly allowed his son to suffer for our sake.

(58) Just think how God makes use of somebody else's wrongdoing to help you! How great is God's wisdom! Who can fathom the depths of his secret ways and the strange paths along which he leads us when he wishes to purify us, to transform us and to deify us!

Chapter 10

Continuation

(59) For the heavenly king to dwell in your soul you must keep it pure and unblemished. For this reason God purifies you like gold in the fire of horrible and painful temptation. When you're distressed and challenged by temptation you will never believe or love more strongly. For the doubts and fears that beset you – whether to believe or not, whether to accept or not – are none other than the kindnesses of love.

(60) And the effects these kindnesses have on you will be clearly apparent and generally result in your having a low opinion of yourself together with a profound awareness of the grandeur of God, and a tremendous confidence that God will protect you from all the risks and dangers, by giving you much greater strength through faith. Additionally, you will realize that it's God himself who gives you the strength to resist the torment of temptation as it's impossible to resist it on your own for a quarter of an hour, so demanding is it at times.

(61) Temptation, then, is your greatest happiness, and when you're most pressed you should rejoice and be at peace rather than sad, and thank God for the favour he's doing you. In the midst of temptations and disgusting thoughts you should calmly pretend to ignore them, as there's nothing more hurtful to the devil than to ignore him and his suggestions. And so you should act as though you haven't heard him and stay calm and not become anxious, or think up lots of replies to him, as there's nothing more treacherous than bandying words with someone who can lead you astray so easily.

(62) To attain sanctity the saints passed along this difficult road of temptation, and the holier they were, the greater the temptation they suffered. Even after they became saints God allowed them to be tempted for their greater glory and to stifle within them the spirit of vanity, so ensuring that they remained safe, humble and alert to their condition.

(63) Finally, the greatest temptation is to be without temptation, and so take heart when it bothers you and resist it with equanimity, for if you wish to serve God and to attain interior peace, you too must pass along this difficult path. Put on your heavy armour, fight the good fight, and allow yourself to be disciplined in this withering fire.

Chapter 11

A definition of interior recollection and how to behave in this state, and on the spiritual war with which the devil tries to unsettle you at this time

(64) Interior recollection is faith and silence in the presence of God. Accustom yourself to this prayer with loving attention, committing yourself to God in reverence and humility, contemplating him without form or image in the depths of your soul, with the general loving awareness of dark faith, allowing no thought or distinction.

(65) You should rest here lovingly and attentively with a simple gaze on God, placing yourself in God's hands without thought of yourself or of perfection. In this state your senses will be obliterated, you will possess interior solitude, and you will enjoy complete obliviousness of the things of this world. Finally, your faith must be pure, simple and all-embracing, without conceptual form or feature.

(66) Interior recollection may be compared to the wrestling that took place all night between God and Jacob, until day broke and God blessed him. You, too, must persevere and struggle unceasingly with the difficulties you encounter during interior recollection, until the light dawns and God gives you his blessing.

(67) You will scarcely have given yourself to God on this interior way when all hell will conspire against you, as just one person inwardly withdrawn in God's presence wages a more effective war against the enemy than a thousand others who journey on the exterior way, for the enemy recognizes the threat that the interior person poses.

(68) When you're recollected God will better appreciate your peace and resignation in the midst of crude and troublesome thoughts than all your good intentions and lofty sentiments. In fact, your own attempts to check such thoughts are a problem in themselves and will make you more anxious. The important thing is gently to ignore them, to accept your own nothingness, and calmly offer up the problem to God.

(69) Although you can't escape the anxiety of thoughts or enjoy

light, consolation, or spiritual comfort, don't worry or abandon your prayer, as such thoughts are the deceits of the enemy. Firmly resign yourself, suffer with patience, and persevere in God's presence, for while you continue like this your interior life will benefit.

(70) You will think that if you feel as empty when you leave your prayer as when you started it, this denotes a lack of preparation on your part and that it hasn't done you any good. You're mistaken in this as the benefit of true prayer doesn't consist in enjoyment of the light or in acquiring knowledge of spiritual matters, for this you can get through discursive thinking without true virtue and perfection. It really consists in suffering patiently and continuing in faith and silence, turning to God with serenity and tranquillity. While you continue like this you have the right attitude and all the preparation you need, and you will improve enormously.

(71) Conflict is very commonplace in this prayer of recollection. On the one hand God will deprive you of the support of the senses to test and discipline you. On the other hand the invisible enemy will harass you with constant suggestions to worry and upset you. Or else you will be troubled by your natural instincts, which are always enemy to the spirit. When you're denied the pleasures of the senses you may feel weak, weary and saddened, so that you dread doing your spiritual exercises, especially your prayer. The urge to give up can be overpowering, what with irritating thoughts, bodily fatigue, falling asleep, and your inability to curb the senses, each of which wants to go its own way. Happy are those who can persevere in all this torment!

(72) St Teresa, the great mystic and teacher, agrees with all this in the letter she wrote to the Bishop of Osma to instruct him in what he should do in prayer when irritating thoughts impinge on the mind: "It is necessary," she says, "to tolerate the nuisance and confusion of irritating thoughts and images and the strength of the appetites. Similarly, you should suffer dryness and disunity as well as the body's inability to submit to the spirit as it should."

(73) All these are called aridities by spiritual people and they're very beneficial if endured with patience, and the person who learns to accept them effortlessly will gain immeasurably from the exercise. When you pray the devil will certainly unleash a war of words to disturb your serenity and to alienate you from this pleasant interior communication by intimidating you into abandoning it, or cause you to think it will be very stressful.

(74) St Teresa says in the same letter: "The birds – that is to say, the forces of evil – peck and pester your mind with irritating thoughts and images and other worries, scattering them hither and thither. Your

heart follows your thoughts and so the benefit of prayer is considerable if you manage to bear these problems and irritations with patience. This means that you must sacrifice yourself in the holocaust of temptation leaving nothing unconsumed in the fire." This is how St Teresa encourages you to resist thoughts and temptations, and as long as you yourself don't succumb to them, the benefit is doubled.

(75) Whenever you try gently to put aside empty thoughts, then God will reward you, and although it may appear that you're doing nothing, rest assured, for God is well pleased with your determination in prayer.

(76) "For to rest there" (concludes St Teresa) "without obvious benefit, is not a waste of time but highly profitable, because you work without self-interest and only for God's glory. Even though you may think you're working in vain, in fact you're like sons who work on their father's estate who although they don't receive a wage at the end of the day, receive what's due to them at the end of the year." This is how St Teresa endorses our teaching with her own.

Chapter 12

Continuation

(77) God doesn't love more those who do more, who feel more, or who show greater emotion, but those who suffer most if they worship God with faith and reverence. It's true that to be deprived of prayer based on the senses or our natural faculties is a harsh penance. But God rejoices and delights in our peace of mind when we're quiet and resigned. Don't revert to vocal prayer at this stage because although it's fine in itself it's an obvious temptation, as the enemy would like you to think that God doesn't speak to you personally when you don't feel emotion, but that you're merely wasting your time.

(78) God doesn't like wordiness but prefers single-mindedness of purpose. God's greatest glory and happiness is best served by your silence, eagerness to please, and humility. Press on, persevere, pray and be silent, for although you won't experience emotion you will find the door to the Void, knowing that you're nothing, that you can do nothing, not even have a good thought.

(79) There are many people who have begun to practise this happy prayer of interior recollection only to abandon it, making the excuse that they take no pleasure in it, that they're wasting their time, that thoughts distract them, that they can't reason, or that it doesn't suit them because they feel no sense of God, whereas in fact they could have trusted, stayed silent and had patience. All this is simply showing ingratitude by going in search of the pleasure of the senses, which is motivated by self-love. They seek themselves rather than God by not accepting a little discomfort and aridity. Yet a small act of reverence in aridity will most surely earn the prize of eternity.

(80) God told the Venerable Mother Francisca López of Valencia, a religious of the Third Order of St Francis, three things of great value regarding interior prayer. First, that a quarter hour of prayer with the senses and faculties recollected does more good than five days of penitential exercises, hairshirts, disciplines, fasting and sleeping on boards, because all this is merely bodily mortification, whereas interior prayer disciplines the soul.

(81) Second, God is more pleased when you commit yourself to an hour's quiet, devout prayer, than when you go on long pilgrimages, as prayer benefits you yourself and those you pray for; additionally, it's a great favour from God and so highly commendable, whereas on a pilgrimage you're distracted and your will is enfeebled, quite apart from other drawbacks.

(82) Third, continual prayer means that you're always committed to God and that in order to follow the interior way you must make progress in the affection of the will rather than exhaust the mind.

(83) The more you delight in the senses, the less God delights in you. To concentrate on God, rejecting thoughts and temptations with the greatest tranquillity you can manage, is a superior method of prayer.

(84) I will conclude this chapter by disabusing you of the common fallacy of those who say that in this interior prayer of quiet you don't use your faculties and that you're idle: this is an obvious mistake of the inexperienced, because although the memory, understanding and reasoning abilities are not involved, the higher intellect certainly is. This operates by direct intuition, guided by faith and the Holy Spirit. Additionally, the will is more concerned with one simple commitment than with many. Moreover, the operations of the will and intellect are so simple, imperceptible and spiritual, that you will hardly be aware of them and much less will you reflect on them.

Chapter 13

What you must do in interior recollection

(85) You must pray so that you may surrender yourself entirely into God's hands with perfect resignation, by making an act of faith, trusting that you are in God's presence, dwelling thereafter in pure tranquillity, equanimity, silence and calm, trying to continue throughout the day, throughout the year and throughout your life in that first commitment to contemplation in faith and love.

(86) There is no need to repeat this commitment, nor to repeat feelings and emotions that have their origins in the senses, for they are a hindrance to the purity of that spiritual and perfect commitment of the will. Apart from the fact that these gentle emotions are imperfect (because of the conscious effort with which they are made, and the self-gratification and consolation that accompany them, by diverting your attention to the senses), there is no need to repeat them, as the mystic Falconi* explains very well with the following metaphor:

(87) "If you have given a precious jewel to a friend, once it has been given there's no need to repeat the act of giving saying each day "Sir, I'm giving you this jewel; Sir, I'm giving you this jewel," but rather let it be, and not wish for it back, for while you don't take it back, or want to take it back, it's always his to keep."

(88) In the same way, having surrendered in loving resignation to the will of God, all you have to do is continue in this way, without making new commitments that derive from the senses, provided you don't take back the jewel of surrender by doing something against God's will when you're engaged in everyday affairs, because in these you're also doing his will and live in continual and virtual prayer. They always pray (said Theophylact) who do good works, and neither do they cease praying except when they cease to be just.

(89) You must therefore reject all things of the senses to achieve stability of spirit and for recollection to become an interior habit, which is so effective that merely the determination to pray reveals the living presence of God. This is the preparation for prayer, or put differently, it is simply a more effective extension of continual prayer, in which contemplatives must establish themselves.

---

*FALCONI, Juan: Seventeenth-century Spanish mystic, sometimes dubbed "prequietist".

Chapter 14

When you're in God's presence, perfectly resigned in pure faith, you're in virtual and acquired contemplation

(99) You will say to me, as many people do, that having resigned yourself in God's presence by the act of pure faith we've mentioned, that you're getting nowhere because your thoughts wander in prayer and you can't concentrate on God.

(100) Don't worry, you're not wasting your time or giving up your prayer because when you're recollected you don't actually need to be thinking of God. It's sufficient to give your attention in the first place, so long as you don't deviate from your plan and go back on your intention, just like those who hear mass and say the divine office are doing their duty by virtue of their initial intention, although subsequently they may not be thinking of God all the time.

(101) St Thomas Aquinas says as much in the following words: "The first intention and thought of God that a person has in prayer is of sufficient value for the duration of the prayer, even though he may have no further thought of God" (2.2.q.82, art.13).

(102) The prayer continues, according to St Thomas, even though the mind wanders in thought, provided you ignore it, or you don't leave your prayer or change your initial intention to be with God. And you certainly won't change it if you stay where you are. You will gather from this that you should persevere although your mind strays with involuntary thoughts. "In spirit and in truth," (says St Thomas) "the person who fully intends to pray, will pray, although through weakness the mind may wander: but unintentional distraction doesn't vitiate the prayer."

(103) But you will ask: shouldn't you at least remember that you're in God's presence and often say to God: "Lord, you're with me, and I want to give myself wholly to you"? I would answer this by saying there's no need, because you've made up your mind to pray and are doing so for that reason. Your faith and intention to pray are sufficient and the simpler you keep it, without words or thoughts, the purer, more spiritual, interior and worthy of God it is.

(104) Isn't it absurd and disrespectful when you're in the king's presence to say to him from time to time: "Lord, I believe your majesty is with me"? It is precisely the same with God. You see God with the eyes of pure faith, you believe in him and you're in his presence, and so when you believe in this way you don't need to say "My God, you're with me," but simply have trust, for when it's time to pray your initial intention will guide you and lead you to contemplate God in pure faith and perfect resignation.

(105) And so, as long as you don't retract this intention, you will always walk in faith and in virtual and acquired contemplation, even though you're unaware of it or don't involve your memory, make fresh commitments, or think discursively. In the same way that Christians, married women and clerics don't make fresh commitments all the time – the first in regard to their baptism: "I'm a Christian"; the second as to their marriage: "I'm married"; and the third concerning their vocation: "I'm a cleric" – nevertheless, the first is still baptized, the second still married, and the third professed. All it means is that Christians must do good works to prove their faith and set greater store by deeds rather than words, married women should demonstrate the fidelity they promised their husbands, and religious give the obedience they owe their superior.

(106) Similarly, those persons on the interior way who have made up their mind that God is with them, and having resigned themselves in his presence, must content themselves with their faith in all activities and exercises, without making new commitments.

Chapter 15

Continuation

(107) These instructions apply not only during prayer but also when it's over, by night and day, and at all times and in all your daily activities. And if you say to me that often during the day you don't remember to renew your commitment, I would reply that although it might appear to you that you've been distracted from it to attend to your daily duties, such as studying, reading, preaching, eating, drinking, doing business, and so on, you're mistaken, because you don't leave it on this account, and neither do you stop doing God's will, or praying, as St Thomas said.

(108) All these activities aren't against God's will or your own resignation as obviously God wants you to eat, study, work, do business, etc., and so by attending to these matters you don't necessarily leave God or abandon your prayer.

(109) However, if when you're in prayer, or away from it, you allow yourself to be distracted, or to be carried away by some emotion or other, you should then turn back to God and renew the act of pure faith and resignation. But you needn't renew this act when you're undergoing aridities, as they're good for you, and, no matter how rigorous they may be, they can't alienate you from God who rests in your faith. Aridities should never be considered a distraction; this amounts to lack of awareness in beginners and absentmindedness in proficients, for when you rest in the Void and accept these aridities patiently, you will enter your innermost centre and God will work miracles in you.

(110) You should try, then, from the time you leave prayer until you return to it, not to let your mind wander, but rather remain totally resigned to God's will, trusting him as a loving father, that he may do with you in all things as he sees fit. Don't ever revoke this intention, for although you may busy yourself with your everyday concerns, you will always be in prayer. In this vein St Chrysostom said: "The just person doesn't stop praying, unless he ceases to be just; he always prays who acts well. The good intention is prayer, and if the intention continues, so does the prayer" (Super I Ad Thessalon. 5).

(111) You will understand all this better with the following metaphor: When people begin walking to Rome, all the steps they take on the way are voluntary,

and they needn't demonstrate their intention with each step, or make a new commitment, saying "I want to go to Rome, I'm going to Rome," because the first commitment to walk to Rome stays with them without the need for them to say it, although they don't walk without wanting to. Moreover, you will find that with just one single commitment these travellers walk, speak, hear, see, reason, eat, and do other things without them interrupting the initial act of the will, or for that matter the actual walking to Rome.

(112) The same thing happens to contemplatives. Having committed themselves to God they continue in this commitment so long as they don't withdraw it, although they occupy themselves in hearing, speaking, eating and other duties and activities during the day. St Thomas Aquinas put all this very succinctly: "A person who has undertaken a journey for God's sake shouldn't have God consciously on his mind, or during any part of the journey" (Contra Gentiles, Bk 3, ch. 238, nos 2, 3).

(113) You might say that all Christians practise this because they all have faith, and even though they aren't interior souls, they can carry out this teaching, especially those who journey by the exterior way of meditation and discursive thought. It's true that all Christians have faith, and especially those who reflect and meditate. But the faith of those who travel on the interior way is very different because it's pure, universal and non-specific, and for that reason more practical, more alive, effective and enlightened, as the Holy Spirit gives most light to those who are best prepared, which is always the case when a person is recollected. The Holy Spirit enlightens you according to your degree of recollection. Although it's true that God imparts some light in meditation, it's faint and is as different to his communication to the mind recollected in pure faith as are two or three drops of water to the ocean. Two or three specific truths are communicated in meditation, whereas in interior recollection and pure faith God's wisdom is an abundant ocean and is freely given in this obscure, simple, general, and universal awareness.

(114) Resignation is also more perfect in these people because it is born of interior and infused strength which increases as the practice of pure faith in silence and resignation is continued. Similarly, the gifts of the Holy Spirit increase in contemplatives. Although these gifts are also found in all those in a state of grace, they are, as it were, lacking in vitality and vigour and very different to the gifts that contemplatives enjoy, by virtue of their light, vitality, and effectiveness.

(115) And so you will understand that interior persons who are in the habit of praying daily at a particular time are constantly in God's presence. This true and important doctrine is taught by all the saints and by all experienced teachers of the mystical life, because they all had the same teacher: the Holy Spirit.

Chapter 16

The way to enter interior recollection by the most holy humanity of Christ, our Lord

(116) There are two kinds of spiritual people totally opposed to one another. Some say that you must always meditate and reflect on the mysteries of Christ's Passion. Others, going to the opposite extreme, say that meditation on the mysteries of the life, Passion and death of the Saviour, isn't prayer, nor even a help to it; that only rapture in God, whose divinity the soul contemplates in quietness and silence, should be called prayer.

(117) It's certain that Christ, our Lord, is the guide, the entrance and the way, as he himself said in his own words: "I am the way and the truth, and the life" (John 14:6). And that before you are to enter God's presence and be united with him you must be cleansed in the precious blood of the Redeemer and be adorned with the wealth of his Passion.

(118) By his teaching and example Christ our Lord is your light, mirror, and guide, the way and only entrance by which to find those pastures of eternal life and the vast ocean of divinity. And so it follows that you don't have to erase completely the memory of the Passion and death of the Saviour. And it also follows that however enraptured you may be, you shouldn't entirely forget his most holy humanity.

(119) But it doesn't follow that when you're practised in interior prayer, and when you can no longer reason, you must always be meditating and reflecting (as those other spiritual people say) on the most holy mysteries of the Saviour. It's holy and good to meditate, and would to God that everyone practised it. And those who meditate with ease, and who reason and reflect, should be left alone in that state and not be moved on to a higher one so long as nourishment and advantage are derived from it.

(120) It's up to God alone, and not the guide, to move you on from meditation to contemplation, because if God doesn't call you with his special grace to this state of prayer, then the guide with all his wisdom and erudition can do nothing.

(121) To take the middle and safest course, then, and to avoid these two extremes that are so opposed, of not completely blotting

out the humanity on the one hand, nor of keeping it constantly in view on the other, let's suggest that there are two ways of considering the holy humanity, which is Christ, our good.

(122) The first is by reflecting on the mysteries and by meditating on the life, Passion and death of our Saviour. The second is by thinking of him intuitively, through pure faith, or through the medium of the memory. When you're making progress in perfection and the interior way through recollection, and having meditated for some time on the mysteries about which you're already informed, then all you have to do is to hold in your mind the faith and love of Christ, and be ready to do for his sake whatever he inspires you to do. In this way you will act according to his teaching, even though you don't always have it in front of you – rather as you would say to a child that he must never desert his father, meaning by this that he needn't keep his eyes constantly fixed on him, but instead hold him always in his memory so that at the right time and place he may attend to his duty.

(123) When you become focused in recollection, then, at the prompting of an experienced guide, you don't need to enter by the first door of meditation on the mysteries, for not only will you be unable to do so without great fatigue to your mind, you don't actually need these meditations as they serve merely as a means to arrive at a faith you already possess.

(124) The noblest, the most spiritual and most appropriate way for those practised in interior recollection to enter by Christ's humanity and to retain his memory, is the second way, by considering his humanity and Passion by a simple act of faith, by loving him and remembering that he is the dwelling place of divinity, the beginning and end of our salvation, and that for our sake he was born, suffered, and died so appallingly.

(125) This, then, is the method that benefits those on the interior way without this holy, sincere, swift, and instantaneous memory of the humanity being an obstacle to the progress of interior recollection, unless, when you start to pray, you're not focused, for then it will be better to continue meditating. Nevertheless, even if you're not focused, the simple and swift remembrance of Christ's humanity will not prevent you from attaining the highest point where you're most enraptured, when you're most void of thought, and transformed.

(126) This is the method favoured by St Teresa for contemplatives and which contradicts the controversial opinions of some schoolmen. This is the safe straight road free from danger, and the one the Lord has taught to many to attain the quiet and tranquillity of contemplation.

(127) When you're focused, then, place yourself at the door of the

divine compassion, which is the gentle and loving memory of the Cross and Passion of the word made flesh, which is Christ who died for our sake. Remain there with humility resigned to the will of God, ready for whatever he has in mind for you. And if from this tender and sincere memory you fall into forgetfulness, there's no need to make a further repetition of it, but rather remain in silence and quiet in the presence of the Lord. How wonderfully St Paul approves of our teaching in the epistle he wrote to the Colossians, in which he urges them and us in whatever we do, in thought or deed, to do it in the name of Jesus Christ and for his love (Col. 3:17). God grant that we all begin with Jesus Christ, and that only in him and by him may we attain perfection.

Chapter 17

On interior and mystical silence

(129) There are three kinds of silence: the first is the silence of words, the second of desires, and the third of thoughts. The first is perfect, the second more perfect, and the third most perfect. With the first, the silence of words, we achieve virtue; with the second, of desires, we attain quiet; with the third, of thoughts, interior recollection. By not speaking, desiring or thinking, we arrive at the true and perfect mystical silence in which God speaks to us, communicates himself to us, and reveals to us in our most intimate depths the most perfect and exalted wisdom.

(130) God calls us and leads us to this interior solitude and mystical silence when he tells us he wishes to speak to us alone, in the most secret and intimate part of our heart. You must enter this mystical silence if you wish to hear the gentle, interior and divine voice. It's not enough for you to give up the world to acquire this treasure, neither is the relinquishing of your desires sufficient, nor detachment from the senses, if you don't detach yourself from all desire and thought. Rest in this mystical silence, and you will open the door for God to communicate with you, to unite you with himself, and to transform you.

(131) Your perfection doesn't consist in speaking or thinking a lot about God, but in loving him greatly. Attain this love through perfect resignation and interior silence. The love of God is all to do with deeds; it has few words. Similarly, St John the Evangelist advises and approves: "My little children, let us not love in words nor with the tongue, but in deeds and truth."

(132) You should now be convinced that perfect love has nothing to do with loving acts in prayer nor with tender outbursts, nor even with those interior commitments by which you tell God that you have infinite love for him and that you love him more than yourself. It may be that when you say this you seek your own self and your own self-love, rather than the true love of God, for love consists in deeds rather than subtle reasoning.

(133) If a rational being is to understand the secret desire and intention of your heart, you have to express it in words. But God, who knows what's in your heart, doesn't need you to explain it and prove it for him. Neither is God impressed, as the Evangelist says, with love expressed in words, but rather with truth and deed. What good is it if you tell God with great earnestness and fervour that you love him tenderly and perfectly above all things, if when you're the victim of some spiteful little remark or slight, you don't resign yourself or allow yourself to be humbled for God's sake. This would obviously prove that your love was in words and not deeds.

(134) You must try to resign yourself in silence in all things, for in this way, without saying that you love God, you will attain to a love that is perfect, quiet, effective and true. St Peter told our Lord with great feeling that he would willingly lay down his life for his sake, but one word from a young girl and he denied him, and his zeal came to nothing (Matt. 26). Mary Magdalen, on the other hand, didn't say a word, but Jesus, enchanted by her perfect love, was fulsome in his praise of her, saying that she loved greatly (Luke 7). It's in your interior life that the most perfect virtues of faith, hope and charity are practised, in the stillness of silence, with no need to tell God you love him, hope and believe in him, because God knows what's in your heart better than you do.

(135) How well the Venerable Gregorio López, that most profound of mystics, understood and practised this act of pure love. His life was one continual prayer, a continuous contemplation, and love for God, so pure and spiritual that it never involved the affections and emotions of the senses.

(136) For the space of three years he uttered the prayer "Thy will be done in time and eternity," repeating it each time he breathed, until God revealed to him the treasure of this pure, continual act of faith and love in silence and resignation. Subsequently he himself said that for the thirty-six years he lived afterwards he always continued in this pure love, never uttering his former prayer again, or anything that derived from the senses. Oh seraphim incarnate, and deified man! How well you were able to penetrate this interior and mystical silence and to distinguish the interior person from the exterior!

Second Book
On obedience to your spiritual father, on excessive fervour, and on interior and exterior discipline

Chapter 1

To overcome the deceits of the enemy the best strategy is to submit to your spiritual father

(1) It's vital to choose a guide experienced in the interior life as God doesn't wish to do for everyone what he did for St Catherine of Siena: that is to say, immediately take them by the hand to show them the mystical way. If a guide is necessary to teach us the ways of nature, how much greater is the need for a teacher in the ways of grace? And if we need one for exterior and worldly matters, won't our need for one be greater for interior and hidden concerns? If we need one for moral, scholastic and descriptive theology, which are obviously taught, won't we need one even more for mystical knowledge, which is secret, hidden and obscure? And if we need one to instruct us in our dealings with people, and for political affairs, won't we need one for our interior dealings with God?

(2) A guide is also necessary to resist and overcome the deceits of the devil. St Augustine gave many reasons why God ordained that luminaries of the faith, and people of similar calibre, should preside over his Church. The main reason was to protect us from the deceits of the enemy, because if we were to allow our own judgment to guide our actions, we would be stumbling by the minute and fall headlong into the abyss, as happens to heretics and the arrogant. If we were to have angels for teachers, they would throw light on the demons who would be transformed into angels of light. But it was God's wish to give us people like ourselves as guides and counsellors. And if the guide is experienced, then he will know all about the subtle deceits of the devil which, being of little substance, disappear as soon as they're brought to light.

(3) Before choosing your guide you must think carefully and pray, because it's a very serious matter and must come from God. Once you've chosen him, however, you should stick with him, except in very exceptional circumstances, such as his inability to understand the paths along which God is leading you, because nobody can teach what they don't know, which is the first rule of philosophy.

(4) And if he doesn't understand spiritual matters, as St Paul says, (1Cor.2:14), it's a question of ignorance, because these have to be understood from a spiritual point of view, and the guide won't have the experience. But the experienced guide sees everything clearly and takes things as they stand. Lack of experience on the guide's part, then, is the principal reason for leaving him and choosing another, because without this experience you won't improve.

(5) Advice is unnecessary to move from a poor position to a good one, but time, prayer and advice are required to move from a good position to the best, because not everything that is best in itself is best for the individual. And neither is everything that's good for one person good for everyone. Some are called to the ordinary and exterior way, others to the interior and extraordinary, and not everyone is at the same level, as the mystical ways are many and varied. Nobody can take a single step along these hidden, interior paths without an experienced guide, because instead of walking straight you will be faced with the precipice.

(6) When you walk in dread along your chosen road and want to be completely free of fear, obedience to an experienced guide is the safest path, because with his interior light he's able to discern clearly what is temptation and what is inspiration. He can also distinguish those interior activities that spring from nature, from the devil, and from you yourself, so you must give your allegiance to someone experienced who can lay bare the attachments, petty idolatry, and bad behaviour that hinder your progress. In this way not only will you free yourself from the deceits of the devil, but you will travel more in one year than you will in a thousand with an inexperienced guide.

(7) The illustrious Father John Tauler tells the story of how the lay person he helped on the road to perfection was disillusioned with the world and keen to become a saint, and had undertaken a lengthy fast, until when he was asleep one night, sick and debilitated, he heard a heavenly voice say to him: "You self-willed man: if you kill yourself before your proper time, you will have cause to regret it." Filled with terror he went off to the desert and told an anchorite about his abstinence and the path he was following and the anchorite, guided by heaven, disabused him of his grievous error. The lay person told

him he was abstaining to please God, and when questioned as to whose advice he was following, he said nobody's, and was told it was an obvious temptation from the devil. His eyes were opened at this point and he saw the error of his ways, and from then on lived according to a guide's advice. He himself then maintained that the guide gave him more light than all the books that had been published.

Chapter 2

Continuation

(8) It's a great advantage to have a teacher of the mystical way instead of books on spirituality, because the practical teacher can tell you what you must do as he goes along, whereas you might read something unsuitable and so miss vital instruction. Additionally, you can acquire a lot of false notions from books on mysticism, leading you to believe you have something you don't really possess, and to think you're more advanced on the mystical way than is the case, which gives rise to a great deal of risk and harm.

(9) One thing for certain is that the frequent reading of mystical texts that have no foundation in practical experience and that are purely speculative, does more harm than good, as they confuse people rather than shedding light. Moreover, such books fill people with ideas that bewilder them because although they contain information about spiritual matters, this comes from outside sources and dulls the senses rather than purifying them for God to take their place. Many people read this speculative literature continually as they don't want to submit themselves to someone who can show them the light. Certainly, if they do submit themselves to an experienced guide, he won't allow this reading, which means they would then progress and not bother with it. You will gather from this that to have an experienced guide who is able to lead and instruct from actual experience, so that you're not misled by the devil and your own judgment, is a source of great comfort and serenity. Not that the reading of spiritual texts in general is to be frowned upon, because in this case we're talking about people who are purely interior and mystical, for whom this book is intended.

(10) All the saints and mystical teachers agree that the safety of the mystically inclined person is best served by submitting whole-heartedly to a guide. As proof of this I would refer you to some words that God spoke to Doña Marina de Escobar. She relates how when she was ill she asked God if she should stay silent and not tell her spiritual father about the extraordinary things that were going through her mind, so as not to bother him. And God replied: "It isn't a good

idea not to tell your spiritual father, for three reasons. First, just as gold is purified in the crucible, and just as the value of precious stones is known by submitting them to the assayer, so too will you be purified and your true value known by submitting yourself to God's minister. Second, to avoid mistakes it's appropriate that matters should be governed by the order that God has taught through his Church, holy scripture, and the doctrine of the saints. Third, the compassion that God shows to his servants and to purified souls should not be concealed but revealed to his Church, to encourage the faithful to serve God and for God to be glorified through them."

(11) She adds the following words: "In keeping with this truth, when my confessor fell ill and instructed me not to tell everything to the confessor acting on his behalf, but only part of it, I complained to God that I had no one with whom to unburden myself. God replied: "You now have someone to make good the failings of your own confessor, so tell him everything that's happening to you." I replied to this: "No, Lord, not that, Lord." "Why not?" God asked. "Because my confessor has told me not to tell him everything, and I have to obey him." God replied to me: "I'm glad you've given me this answer, and I told you what I did to hear you say it. Do as you were told and tell him a just a few things as you were instructed." "

(12) What St Teresa said about herself is also very much to the point: "Whenever God instructed me to do something, if my confessor said something else, God would speak again and tell me to obey him. Then God would change the confessor's mind, so that he would come back and tell me to do the opposite." (Life, Ch 26). This is the sound and reassuring teaching that keeps at bay the deceits of the devil.

Chapter 3

Excessive fervour and love for others can hinder interior peace

(13) There's no sacrifice more pleasing to God (says St Gregory) than a person's burning zeal to help others. Our eternal father sent his son, Jesus Christ, to the world to carry out this ministry, and ever since it has counted among the most noble and sublime of callings. But if the zeal is excessive, it's a notable hindrance to the ascent of the spirit.

(14) As soon as you're newly filled with the light of fervour then you will want to use it for other people's benefit, and you then run the great risk that what appears to be pure enthusiasm is your own self-love. This zeal perhaps usually comes disguised as excessive enthusiasm, empty self-indulgence, busy affectation, and love of self, all inimical to your peace of mind.

(15) It's never a good idea to love others to the detriment of your spiritual welfare. To please God with simplicity should be your only objective and concern; try to moderate excessive fervour so that tranquillity and interior peace may reign in your soul. Real enthusiasm should express itself as pure love for God, which is genuine and effective love, and a love that works miracles in you, albeit very softly.

(16) In the first instance St Paul encouraged concern for our own soul rather than for others: "Keep a close watch on yourself and your teaching," he said in his epistle (1 Tim. 4:16). Don't strain yourself to make progress, however, for when the time is right and you can be of some help to others, God will help you and give you a suitable task. This worry is God's alone while your job is to rest in tranquillity, detached and completely resigned in God. Don't think you're idle in this state; those who concentrate on doing God's will in all things are doing a great deal. And those who attend to themselves for God's sake do all they should, because one act of complete resignation is worth more than a hundred, or even a thousand, exercises of your own volition.

(17) Although the cistern can contain a lot of water, it will never do so until the sky fills it with rain. Stay quiet, blessed soul, stay quiet, humble and resigned in everything God has in mind for you. Leave

the worry to God, because like a loving father he knows what's best for you. Act in total conformity with God's will, where perfection resides, for those who act according to his will are the mother, son and brother of the son of God himself.

(18) Don't think that God appreciates more those who do most. The one who is loved more is the one who is most humble, faithful and resigned, and most responsive to God's interior inspiration and divine will.

Chapter 4

Continuation

(19) Let all your desires be in conformity with God's will, for God can make streams of water flow from a dry stone, and is displeased with those people who help others prematurely. In this they're mistaken, allowing themselves to be carried away by excessive zeal and empty self-satisfaction.

(20) This is like the disciple of Elisha who was sent by the prophet to revive a corpse with his staff and who was ineffectual because of his conceit, and was then censured by Elisha. Cain was also reproached for his sacrifice, the first in the world to be offered to God, as he too preened himself over the advantage of being the first, and before his father Adam, in offering sacrifice to God.

(21) Even Christ's disciples were guilty of this weakness, taking empty pleasure in casting out the demons, and for this they were severely reprimanded by Jesus. And before Paul preached to the Gentiles and spread the good news about God's kingdom, being then the chosen bearer, citizen of heaven and elect of God for this ministry, it was necessary to test and humble him by having him locked up in prison. Would you want to be a preacher without having passed the test of man and the devil? And would you want to undertake such a responsible ministry and be of help without having passed through the fire of temptation, adversity and passive purification?

(22) It's more important for you to stay quiet and resigned in holy idleness than to undertake important matters by yourself. Don't think that the heroic actions of the great servants of God were the result of their own efforts, because all things, spiritual and temporal, are ordained from eternity by divine providence, including the movement of the smallest leaf. The person who does God's will does everything. And this you must seek in serenity with perfect resignation, accepting everything God has in mind for you. Realize that you're as unworthy of such a high calling as you are of carrying alms to heaven, and in this way you won't prevent quiet in your soul, interior peace, or your divine progress.

Chapter 5

Light, experience, and divine vocation are necessary to guide souls on the interior way

(23) It might seem to you – and to your great satisfaction – that you're cut out to be a guide on the spiritual way. Perhaps you will be driven by hidden arrogance, or blind spiritual ambition. It has to be said, though, that this high calling requires superior light, total detachment and other qualities I'll mention in the following chapters. The grace of vocation is necessary, without which everything is vanity, self-satisfaction and self-interest. Although to lead and guide people to contemplation and perfection is holy and good, how do you know that God wants you for this position? And even if you do know (which isn't easy) that you have great light and experience, what evidence do you have that God wants you for this responsibility?

(24) It's a ministry of quality that we should never undertake until God gives it to us through our superiors or spiritual guides. Even if we managed to be of some benefit to others it would be of serious detriment to ourselves. What good is it if we gain the world for God but lose our own soul? (Matt. 16).

(25) Even though you have clear evidence that you're endowed with interior light and experience, the most important thing is to rest in the Void, quiet and resigned, until God calls you to help others. It's up to God alone, who knows whether you're sufficiently competent and detached. It's not up to you to make this decision or put yourself forward for this ministry, because if you're influenced by your own opinion, self-love will blind and deceive you in such a weighty matter as this.

(26) If vocation is lacking as well as competence, light and experience, then competence, interior light, and experience without vocation are doubly unhelpful. These gifts are not given to everybody, but only to the detached, the resigned, and to those who have attained perfect annihilation through passive purification and suffering in prayer. Don't delude yourself, blessed soul, for if all aspects of this responsibility aren't inspired by genuine zeal, and born of pure love and a purified spirit, then they're disguised as vanity, self-love and spiritual ambition.

(27) How many people full of themselves undertake this ministry

out of self-love, and, instead of pleasing God by becoming empty and detached, become filled with earth, straw, and their own self-righteousness, even though they may be of some benefit to others! Stay quiet and resigned, ignore your own judgment and desires, recognize your inadequacy and sink into the Void, for only in the Void will you find God, true light, your happiness and the greatest perfection.

Chapter 6

Instruction and advice to confessors and spiritual guides

(28) The most important and beneficial ministry is that of confessor and spiritual director, and this is the one that can do irreparable harm if it's not carried out skilfully.

(29) It would be sensible to choose an expert for such a high calling, and one who is naturally inclined to interior prayer.

(30) The first and soundest advice is for him to attain continuous interior recollection, and with this he will succeed in all the exercises and duties connected with his position and vocation, especially those of the confessional, because the recollected person who undertakes necessary exterior duties will find that God makes his presence felt in them and shines through them.

(31) Instruction isn't necessary for those already leading the interior life, only a gentle and tactful removal of those obstructions that hinder God's influence. But it will be necessary to influence them with that holy advice of "secretum meum mihi." Many people think that all confessors are capable of dealing with spiritual matters, which apart from being untrue, means that great harm is done by them when they try to pass on this knowledge without the necessary expertise. Although God may have led them to the interior way, they will be unfamiliar with it and be unable to give proper advice because of their inexperience. On the contrary, they will hinder progress toward contemplation, forcing people to meditate even though they can't, with the result that they confuse and befuddle them instead of helping them, because God wants them to move on to contemplation and they insist on them meditating because they don't know any other way.

(32) To be of benefit you mustn't go looking for people to guide: let them come to you and don't take just anybody, especially women, because usually they don't come well enough prepared. The most effective way is not to set yourself up as a teacher or want to appear as one.

(33) The confessor should use the term "daughter" as little as possible, because it's extremely dangerous as it's so affectionate and God is so jealous.

(34) The jobs the confessor should allow himself away from the confessional should be few in number, because God doesn't want him as a business agent. And if possible he should be seen only in the confessional.

(35) At no time should he be a godfather or executor, as this carries with it a lot of worries inimical to the effectiveness of such a high calling.

(36) The confessor or spiritual guide should never visit spiritual daughters, not even in cases of illness, unless specifically requested by the sick person.

(37) If the confessor seeks interior or exterior retreat, his words will be like burning coals, though he may be unaware of it.

(38) His reproaches in the confessional should usually be mild, although in the pulpit they should be severe. He should be like an angry lion here but in the confessional he should appear as gentle as a lamb. How effective is a mild reproof for penitents! In the confessional they're already contrite, whereas it's necessary to frighten them in the pulpit on account of their blindness and obstinacy. But those who come ill-prepared and demanding absolution should be put right and harshly rebuked.

(39) After doing what he can to help, he shouldn't admire his work because the devil will cunningly allow him to think that what comes from God is all his own doing, when in fact it proceeds from his own self-love, the principal enemy of the self-annihilation that he should strive for to die spiritually.

(40) Although he may often find that people aren't making progress and that proficients may be backsliding, he should keep his interior peace, like the guardian angels. He should be encouraged by this disappointment as perhaps God allows it, among other things, to humble him.

(41) The confessor should avoid, and make those he guides avoid, distraction by external matters, as they're hateful to God.

(42) Although he shouldn't order people to take communion, nor take away this right as a test or discipline, given that there are so many other ways of testing and disciplining, nevertheless communion should not be infrequent for those genuinely motivated, because Jesus didn't allow himself to be enclosed.

(43) Experience shows that if the penance is too harsh it will not be complied with. It's always better for it to be moderate and meaningful.

(44) If the spiritual father appears to show greater interest in one particular daughter it will cause the others a great deal of anxiety. The important thing here is tolerance and tact, and not to give special

praise to anyone as the devil is adept at sowing discord in the guide and will make use of his words to upset the other spiritual daughters.

(45) Purely mystical souls should be mainly concerned with their interior life, while the guide should quietly try to destroy their self-regard and to encourage in them the patience to bear with the interior disciplines with which God annihilates, purifies and perfects them.

(46) The desire for revelations is normally a great obstacle for those leading the interior life, especially women, and there's no natural dream they don't dignify with the name of vision. All these obstacles are to be deplored.

(47) Although silence in matters dictated by the director is difficult for women, nonetheless he must insist on it because it's not right that what's inspired by God should be cause for censure.

Chapter 7

Continuation, exposing the attachments that some confessors and spiritual guides usually have, and a description of the qualities required for the practice of confession and to guide people on the mystical way

(48) The confessor should encourage penitents in prayer, especially when they come to him frequently and he recognizes in them the desire for spiritual well-being.

(49) The golden rule that the confessor must observe to save him from disgrace is on no account to accept gifts.

(50) Although there are many confessors, they're not all good, as some of them know very little. Others are very ignorant; some seek praise from the nobility; others look for favours or presents from their penitents; some, full of spiritual ambition, seek acclaim, and try to attract a lot of penitents; others make a show of their erudition and teaching; others set store by the visions and revelations of their penitents, and instead of dismissing such visions (the only way to keep them humble and unencumbered), praise them and get penitents to write them down to show them off, and to cause a stir. All this is self-love in directors and arrests spiritual progress, because certainly all these considerations and attachments are a hindrance to the effectiveness of their work, which requires total detachment, and whose sole aim should be the glory of God.

(51) There are other confessors who naïvely and arbitrarily believe and praise everybody. Others, going to a harsh extreme, condemn unreservedly all visions and revelations. They're not all to be believed, but they shouldn't all be condemned. There are others who are so enamoured of their female penitents that whatever they dream up, however misguided it is, they venerate it like the holy mysteries. What a great deal of misery this causes the Church!

(52) There are other confessors full of worldly charm and with scant regard for the sanctity of the confessional, and who talk about shallow and unnecessary matters that are far removed from the

decency required by the holy sacrament and the correct attitude to receive its divine grace. And it may happen that a lot of penitents who are waiting to confess, full of their own and domestic affairs, encounter an excessive and unwarranted delay, and become irritated, depressed and impatient, losing the frame of mind that they came with to receive such a holy sacrament.

(53) You still find some good confessors, but to guide people on the mystical way there are so few that John of Avila said there wasn't one in a thousand, and St Francis de Sales one in ten thousand. And the illustrious Tauler said that among a hundred thousand you wouldn't find one experienced spiritual teacher, which is the reason why so few are able to receive mystical knowledge: "Pauci ad eam recipiendam se disponunt," said Henry Arphio (Bk 3, part 3, ch. 22). Would to God this were not true, as there wouldn't be so many wrongs in the world and there would be more saints and fewer sinners.

(54) When the spiritual guide really wants everyone to love virtue, and when the love he has for God is pure and perfect, then with few words and even fewer reasons, he will be very effective.

(55) If interior persons who are undergoing purgation of the passions, and who are withdrawn in prayer, don't have an experienced guide to restrain their intense desire to withdraw and remain in solitude, then they will be rendered incapable of confession, preaching and study, or unable even to engage in those affairs proper to their position and calling.

(56) The experienced guide, then, must watch very carefully when people's faculties begin to be absorbed in God, and not give too much scope for retreat into solitude. He should advise such people not to neglect the responsibilities of their position, such as study or other activities, as long as these are not opposed to their prayer, even though they may appear to distract them, because they will become so absorbed in solitude, so withdrawn in retreat, and alienated so thoroughly from external affairs, that afterwards, if they apply themselves to their work once more, they will do so wearily, with repugnance, and to the detriment of their faculties and brain.

(57) But if the guide is not experienced, he won't know at what point abstraction begins, and at the same time, believing he is giving good advice, will encourage people to go into retreat, where they will be lost. How important it is for the guide to be experienced in the spiritual and mystical way!

Chapter 8

Continuation

(58) Those who guide people without the necessary experience proceed blindly, and fail to understand the various conditions of the soul or its interior and supernatural operations. They only get to know that sometimes the soul is healthy and has light, and that at other times it's in darkness. But as for determining the actual state of the soul and the root cause of its changes, they have no idea, and neither can they find out from books if they haven't experienced these changes in themselves, which is the forge where genuine and actual light is wrought.

(59) If the guide himself hasn't passed along the hidden and painful paths of the interior way, how can he possibly understand or approve? It will be nothing short of a miracle if people find a single experienced guide to encourage them in their insuperable difficulties, and to reassure them over the continual doubts that crop up on the way. Additionally, they will never reach the summit of the holy and blessed mount of perfection without a unique and extraordinary grace.

(60) The guide who is detached should prefer interior solitude to the direction of souls, and if a spiritual teacher has regrets when someone leaves him for another guide, then this is a clear indication that he's not detached or single-mindedly seeking God's glory, but that he's looking to enhance his own reputation.

(61) Similar harm is done when the teacher in an underhand way attracts to himself a person who is under the direction of someone else. This is obviously wrong, because if he believes he's better than another guide, then it's arrogance; and if he knows he isn't as good, then he's a traitor to God, to the person he guides, and to himself, on account of the malicious damage he does to everyone.

(62) Another big fault in spiritual directors is that they won't allow the people they're directing to consult another guide, even though he may be more learned, experienced and spiritually advanced than they are. All this is attachment and love of self. They won't allow people this relief for fear of losing them, and lest it be said that their charges are seeking satisfaction from others that they

can't give themselves. And for the most part they hinder people's progress by these means.

(63) The guide who has heard God's interior voice, and passed through the trials and tribulations of passive purification, is freed from these and many other attachments, for God's interior voice has many and wonderful effects on souls that yield to it, listen to it, and experience it.

(64) It's so effective that the guide will eschew worldly honour, self-love, spiritual ambition, the hankering after acclaim, the desire to be important, the presumption of being the only one, and the belief that a guide knows it all. He will also eschew excessive love of the confessional, and the unbridled desire to direct others on the assumption that he has the necessary expertise. Additionally, he will completely eschew self-regard, presumptuousness, authority, any dwelling on the effect that the guide may produce, or any boasting about penitents' letters and the displaying of them to show the extent of his expertise. And it forestalls envy of other guides and the desire for everyone to come to their own confessional.

(65) Finally, God's interior voice in the soul of the director encourages self-disdain, solitude, silence and obliviousness of friends, relatives and penitents, of whom he is unmindful, unless they speak to him. This is the only way to gauge the teacher's detachment, for he will be more effective when silent than thousands of others, however knowledgeable they may be.

Chapter 9

How simple and prompt obedience is the only means to journey safely along the interior way and to attain interior peace

(66) If you're really intent on denying your own self-will and doing God's will in all things, obedience is absolutely vital, whether it be through the indissoluble bond of the vow you've made to your superior, or the frank acceptance of the direction of an experienced spiritual guide with the qualities described in the preceding chapters.

(67) You will never reach the peak of the mountain of perfection, or the high throne of interior peace, if you're governed by self-will. You must overcome this cruel and fierce enemy of God and yourself. Like rebels, your own judgment must be subdued, eradicated and consumed in the fire of obedience. This fire will be your touchstone to decide whether it's God's will or your own that you're following: the last drop of self-will must be annihilated in this holocaust.

(68) An ordinary life of obedience is of greater value than one in which you apply hefty penances to yourself. This is because apart from being free from the deceits of the devil, obedience is the truest holocaust in which you sacrifice yourself to God on the altar of your heart. It was for this reason that a great servant of God said that he would rather pick up dung through obedience than be caught up into the third heaven through his own self-will.

(69) Obedience is the comprehensive means to attain perfection quickly. It's impossible for you to attain real peace in your heart if you don't deny yourself and subdue your self-will. And to do this, the way forward is single-mindedly to obey the person who is acting on God's behalf: "Effundite coram illo corda vestra" (Ps. 61). For everything that you utter with genuine submission to your spiritual father leaves your heart free, secure and blameless. The most effective method to advance on the spiritual way, then, is to believe whole-heartedly that your spiritual director is in God's place, and that whatever he says and instructs is said and instructed by God.

(70) God said on many occasions to the Venerable Sister Ana María

de San José, discalced Franciscan: "I would rather you obeyed your spiritual father than me." And God said to the Venerable Sister Catalina Paluci one day: "You should go sincerely and honestly to your spiritual father, as if you were coming to me, without bothering whether or not he is competent. You have only to believe that he's directed by the Holy Spirit and that he's in my place. When you believe this I will never allow you to be misled by him." What blessed words, so worthy of being impressed on the hearts of those who wish to advance along the road to perfection!

(71) Doña María de Escobar said that if in her opinion Jesus instructed her to take communion and her spiritual father forbade it, then she felt obliged to obey her spiritual father. This was because a saint came down from heaven to give her the reason, and this was that she might be mistaken in the first place, but not in the second.

(72) The Holy Spirit advises everyone in Proverbs that we take advice and don't trust our own judgment: "Ne innitaris prudentiae tuae" (Prov. 3). And Tobias says that to be on the safe side we should never be guided by our own judgment, but always seek another's opinion: "Consilium semper a sapiente perquire" (4:19). Although the spiritual father may err in his advice, you can't be mistaken in following him, because you're doing the right thing: "Qui judicio alterius operatur, prudenter operatur." And God doesn't give licence to directors to uphold, even by miraculous means, the visible court of the spiritual father, where you know for certain God's will resides.

(73) Apart from the fact that this teaching is common to all the saints, Jesus himself approved of it when he said that spiritual fathers should be heard and obeyed just like himself: "Qui vos audit me audit" (Luke 10). And this is the case even when their deeds don't correspond to their words and advice, as we see from St Matthew: "Quocumque dixerint vobis facite, secundum autem opera eorum nolite facere" (23:1).

Chapter 10

Continuation

(74) According to St Gregory, the person who submits in holy obedience possesses all the virtues. And so, God rewards your humility and obedience, and teaches and enlightens your guide, to whose direction you should always submit, as he stands in God's place. In this way your thoughts, deeds, inclinations, inspirations and temptations will be exposed freely, clearly, faithfully and simply. Additionally, the devil can't deceive you and you will be sure to give an account of yourself to God, without fear, for the things you do and those you omit to do. And so those who want to travel without a guide are very close to being deluded – if they're not already – because temptation will seem inspiration to them.

(75) You should know that to be perfect it's not enough to honour and obey your superiors; it's also necessary to honour and obey inferiors.

(76) For obedience to be perfect it must be voluntary, pure, prompt, happy, interior, blind, and persevering: voluntary, without fear or force; pure, without worldly interest, respect, or self-love, but purely for God's sake; prompt, without reply, excuse or delay; happy, without interior friction, and with diligence; interior, as exterior obedience alone won't do, but the heart and spirit must be involved also; blind, free from your own judgment, subjecting this to the guide who directs you, without looking for intention, objective, or reason for the obedience; persevering, with firmness and consistency until death.

(77) "Obedience," says St Bonaventure, "should be prompt, without delay; devout, without arrogance; voluntary, without contradiction; simple, without examination; persevering, without pause; ordered, without deviation; pleasant, without trouble; courageous, without hesitation; and universal, without exception." Remember, blessed soul, if you want to do God's will diligently, the only way is through obedience: those who want to be their own director are deceiving themselves, and although they feel strongly that a good spirit is speaking to them, if they don't submit to the judgment of the spiritual director, then the communication may as well come from the devil. Gerson said as much, as did many other spiritual teachers.

(78) This teaching can be verified by the case of St Teresa. When Teresa saw that Doña Catalina was performing a harsh penance in the wilderness, she decided to imitate her, against the advice of her spiritual father, who forbade it. At this point God said to her: "Don't do that, my child; you're fine as you are. You see all the penance that Dona Catalina is doing: well, I think more of your obedience" (Life). From that time she made a vow to obey her spiritual father. And in chapter 26 she relates how God told her many times not to forget to open her heart to her spiritual father and tell him of the graces she had received, and obey him in everything.

(79) You can see now how it has been God's wish to have this important teaching confirmed in the scriptures, by the saints, by Doctors of the Church, and by reason and example, in order to root out entirely the deceits of the enemy.

Chapter 11

When, and in which matters, it's important for you to profess obedience

(80) So that you know when obedience is most necessary, I should like to advise you that when you're prey to the horrible and unseemly suggestions of the enemy, when you're suffering most from darkness, anguish, aridities and helplessness, when you're under most pressure from the temptations of anger, rage, blasphemy, lust, cursing, weariness, desperation, impatience and desolation, then this is precisely the time to believe and obey the experienced director. With his holy advice he will pacify you so that you don't get carried away by the insistent promptings of the enemy, who will lead you to believe that in this distress and abandonment you're lost, that God hates you, that you're in disgrace, and that obedience is no longer of benefit.

(81) You will feel hemmed in by distressing scruples, regrets, worries, problems, torments, mistrust. You will feel alienated from worldly comforts, and suffer troubles that are so severe that your grief will seem inconsolable. O blessed soul, how happy you will be if you trust your guide, if you submit to him and obey him. If you do this you will travel safely along the hidden and interior path of the dark night, even though you will feel you've lost your way, that you're worse off than ever, that you can find only abomination and signs of condemnation in your heart.

(82) You will judge from the available evidence that you're possessed by the devil, because the results of your interior work and the awful distress you suffer can be confused with the painful invasion of spirits and demons. Maintain a firm belief in your guide during this time because your greatest happiness will come from your obedience.

(83) You should beware, then, that when the devil sees people deny themselves completely and submit to their director, he usually lets loose all hell to prevent this infinite good and holy sacrifice. Consumed with rage and jealousy he will sow discord between the two of you, causing you to feel weariness, annoyance, aversion, repugnance, distrust and hatred of the guide, and perhaps even take advantage of your tongue to insult him. But if he's experienced he will laugh at these subtle

deceits of the devil. And although the devil will try with various suggestions to persuade you in this state not to believe your director, so that you don't obey him or make progress, nevertheless you must believe it's sufficient to obey, albeit without self-satisfaction.

(84) You may ask for some tolerance from your guide, or you will tell him of some special grace you have received. If he doesn't allow you any latitude, or disabuses you of your special grace, so that you don't become conceited, and then you go against his advice, or leave him, then it's an indication that the grace was false and that your spirit is at risk. But if you trust and obey, even though you feel it keenly, it's an indication that you're alert but poorly disciplined. However, if you continue with this harsh medicine, even though your inferior self is disturbed and resentful, your superior self will welcome the medicine, as basically you would like to be humbled and disciplined, because you know this is God's will. And although you may not be aware of it, your guide will be increasingly pleased with you.

(85) The way to deny self-love and your own opinion is to accept completely the advice of the spiritual doctor. If he stops you from doing what you like, or tells you to do what you don't want to do, then a thousand spurious reasons will come to mind to reject his good advice. You will then realize your spirit is not entirely disciplined and that self-love has not been eradicated, which is the principal enemy of prompt obedience and peace of mind.

(86) It's essential to conquer yourself, to overcome your strong feelings, and to scorn these spurious reasons, by obeying, staying silent, and following the good advice of the director, because in this way you will suppress your appetites and self-love.

(87) For this reason the ancient Fathers, as experienced spiritual teachers, tested their disciples by various and extraordinary methods: they instructed some to plant lettuce over their eyes, and others to water dry tree trunks, and yet others to sew and unsew their clothes all the time. All these are marvellous and effective ruses to test simple obedience and to cut at the root of the weed of self-love.

Chapter 12

Continuation

(88) You must realize you won't take one step on the spiritual way if you don't try to conquer this fierce enemy, self-love, and the person who doesn't recognize this danger will never be cured. Sick people who understand their illness know for sure that although they're thirsty, it's not right for them to drink, and that the medicine, although bitter, is good for them. For this reason they don't trust their appetite, or their own judgment, but put themselves in the care of an experienced doctor and follow his instructions completely as the means to their cure. Recognizing that they're ill helps them not to rely on themselves but to follow the sound advice of the doctor.

(89) We're all of us sick with the malady of self-love; we're all full of ourselves; we yearn only for what does us harm, and what does us good displeases and upsets us. It's vital, then, to adopt the cure of sick people who want to get better, which is not to trust our own whim and fancy, but to accept the sound advice of the experienced spiritual doctor, without objection or excuse, scorning the bogus pleadings of self-love. If we obey in this way we'll certainly get better and conquer self-love, which is the enemy of peace, quiet, perfection and the spirit.

(90) How many times have you been misled by your own judgment? And how many times have you changed your mind out of shame for having believed yourself? If someone has deceived you two or three times, you wouldn't trust him again, so why trust your own judgment when you've been deceived so often? Don't trust it, blessed soul, don't trust it; submit completely and follow with blind obedience.

(91) You will be very content when you have an experienced guide, and even very happy, but it will be of no consequence if you set store by your own judgment rather than his advice, and don't submit completely to him in all truth and sincerity.

(92) An important person suffering from a serious illness has a famous and experienced doctor in his house who diagnoses the pain and its causes, nature and condition, and knowing for certain that the

illness can be cured with vigorous cauterization, instead orders palliatives. Isn't this very silly? If he knows that the palliative is of little use and that cauterization is effective, why doesn't he apply it? For the simple reason that although the sick person wants to get better, the doctor has the full picture and knows he isn't up to taking strong medicines, and so he orders the cautious use of palliatives, because although he doesn't effect a cure with them, he saves the patient's life by stabilizing him.

(93) What good is it if you have the best director in the world if you don't truly submit? Although he may be experienced and understand your illness and know which remedy to apply, he doesn't administer the most effective medicine to counter your self-will because he understands the condition of your spirit, which isn't prepared for the rooting out of self-centredness. And so you will never be cured, and it will be a miracle if you stay in a state of grace with such a fierce enemy within you.

(94) If your guide is experienced, he will have contempt for all your claims to favours from God if your spirit is not well established. Trust and obey him by following his advice, because if your spirit is not genuine, but of the devil, your hidden pride, which is the work of the devil who counterfeits the spirit, will be revealed.

(95) If you like to be praised and would like to broadcast the favours you receive from God, and you don't trust and obey the director who disparages such favours, then everything is a lie, and the angel a demon in disguise. When a person sees that the experienced guide has a low opinion of these deceits, if his spirit is bad, he will withdraw his affection from him and try gradually to distance himself and look for somebody else to deceive, because pride never keeps company with someone out to humble it. On the contrary, if the spirit is genuine and of God, these tests have the effect of increasing love and steadfastness, and a person will tolerate them and seek more of them. In this way we can gauge unequivocally the stability of the spirit.

Chapter 13

Frequent communion is an effective method of acquiring all the virtues, and especially interior peace

(96) Four things are necessary to attain perfection and interior peace. The first is prayer, the second obedience, the third frequent communion, and the fourth interior discipline. Now that we've dealt with prayer and obedience, it will be as well to deal with communion.

(97) There are many people who deprive themselves of the tremendous value of this precious nourishment as they think they're not sufficiently prepared and they need an angelic purity. If you're sincere and have a genuine desire to do God's will, without wanting a devotion based on the senses or your own self-will, then go forward with confidence, for you're well prepared.

(98) All difficulties, scruples, temptations, doubts, fears, misgivings and contradictions must be broken on this rock of desire to do God's will. And although the best preparation is frequent communion, for one communion prepares you for another, I want nevertheless to show you two sorts of preparation. The first is for exterior souls who are willing and able, the second for spiritual persons who live the interior life and who have more light and knowledge of God, his mysteries, his mode of operation and sacraments.

(99) The preparation for exterior souls is to take confession, withdraw from the world before communion, remain in silence, and consider what it is they're about to receive, and who is receiving it, and that it's going to be the most important thing in the world, which is to receive almighty God. What a wonderful favour it is to receive purity in defilement, grandeur in abjectness, and for the creature to receive from the creator!

(100) The second preparation, which is for interior and spiritual souls, is to try to live with more purity, with greater self-denial, with total detachment, with interior discipline and continuous recollection. If you journey in this way you don't actually need to prepare yourself, because your life is a continual and perfect preparation.

(101) If you don't recognize these virtues in yourself, then for the same reason you should take communion frequently to acquire them.

Don't let the fact that you feel dry, inadequate and cold put you off, because frequent communion is the medicine that cures ailments and increases virtue. Similarly, when you're sick you go to the doctor, and when you're cold you draw near to the fire.

(102) If you come to communion with humility and with a desire to do God's will, and have your confessor's permission, you can take it every day, and every day you will improve and benefit. Don't worry if you lack a love that is warm and based on the senses, because this sort of love is not perfect and is usually given to weak and delicate souls.

(103) You will say that you feel ill-prepared, that you lack devotion and enthusiasm, and even that you don't feel like communion, so how can you take it frequently? Rest assured that none of this will stop you or do you any harm, so long as you have a firm intention not to sin and are determined to avoid any kind of offence. And if you confess to all those offences you can recall, you should be in no doubt that you're well prepared for holy communion.

Chapter 14

Continuation

(104) In this ineffable sacrament you join with Christ to become one with him, which is the highest and most admirable grace, and one worthy of every respect and gratitude. Christ's beneficence in becoming man was immense, and his goodness was even greater to die so ignominiously on the Cross for our sake. But to give himself utterly to us in this wonderful sacrament is beyond comparison. Herein consists his remarkable gift to us, for after this there's nothing more to give, and nothing more to receive. If only we could comprehend him! If only we could understand him!

(105) To think that God, being who he is, should want to communicate himself to me! To think that God wishes to forge a mutual bond with me, so unworthy am I! How blessed we are to eat at this heavenly table! How blessed we are to be consumed in this burning bush! If only we could all become one in spirit with our sovereign lord! Who is leading us astray? Who is preventing us from being consumed like the salamander in the divine fire of this holy table?

(106) It's true, oh Lord, that you come to me, a miserable creature, but it's also true that you dwell within yourself, in your glory, and in your splendour. Take me to yourself, oh my Jesus, in your beauty and majesty, for I am supremely happy that my unworthiness cannot sully your beauty. Abide with me while dwelling within yourself, dwell in all your splendour and magnificence, even though you abide in my darkness and misery.

(107) Oh my soul, how great is your depravity, how great your poverty! What is man, oh Lord, that you should remember him in this way, that you should come to him, and exalt him? (Job 7:17). What is man that you should hold him in such high regard, wishing to delight in him, and abide in him personally in all your grandeur? How, Lord, can such a miserable creature receive your infinite majesty? Humble yourself, oh my soul, in the depths of the Void. Confess your unworthiness, look upon your misery, and acknowledge the miracle of the divine love that allows itself to be corrupted in this incomprehensible mystery, that it may communicate itself and unite itself with you.

(108) Oh, grandeur of love! To think that loving Jesus could be

contained in a little host! To think that this great lord should be imprisoned out of love for me! That he should become in his own fashion a slave to us, giving himself over completely and sacrificing himself to the eternal Father for our sake! Oh heavenly slave, bind my heart that it may never be free again, until totally annihilated it dies to the world and lives united with you!

(109) If you wish to acquire all the virtues in great measure then draw near blessed soul, draw near frequently to this most holy table, for there do all the virtues reside. Eat, oh soul, of this heavenly food, eat and persevere, draw near with humility, come in faith to partake of the heavenly bread, for it is the soul's target from which love draws its arrows, saying: come, oh soul, and eat this delicious food if you wish to attain purity, charity, light, strength, peace and perfection.

Chapter 15

When you ought to use exterior and bodily penances, and how harmful they are when used indiscreetly according to your own judgment

(110) There are some people who take great pains to achieve sanctity and who then go backwards when they apply indiscreet penances to themselves. They're like those who try to sing more than their strength will allow, and who strain themselves till they're tired, and instead of doing better, do worse.

(111) Many have fallen foul of this obstacle as they should have surrendered their judgment to their spiritual father. They prefer to believe, however, that if they don't take harsh penances upon themselves they will never be saints, as if sanctity consisted only in penances. They will tell you that whoever sows little, reaps little, but in fact the only seed they sow with indiscreet penance is the seed of self-love, which they should be trying to root out.

(112) The worse thing about indiscreet penances is that those who use these dry and sterile austerities actually engender and make natural a certain bitterness toward themselves and others, which is far removed from the true spirit. They are bitter toward themselves because they don't experience the gentleness of Christ's Cross, or the sweetness of charity, but only the harshness of penances, which leaves them embittered. They're then bitter toward others, often noting their failings and reproaching them, or criticizing their imperfections and shortcomings when they see them following a regime less rigid than their own. These exercises and penances give rise to selfish pride when they see how few there are who do them, and then they think they're better than everyone else, which leads to a real loss of virtue. Consequently they feel envious of others when they see they're more favoured by God while doing fewer penances, which is a clear indication that they're putting their trust in their own efforts.

(113) Prayer is the soul's nourishment, and the soul of prayer is interior discipline. Although bodily penance and all the other exercises with which the flesh is punished are good, holy and laudable (when

done in moderation, and in keeping with each person's state and condition, and under the guide's direction), nevertheless, you will never gain any virtue by these means. On the contrary, if they don't grow from within, then you're pandering to empty vanity. You should now be aware of the right time when you should mainly apply exterior penances.

(114) When you begin to withdraw from the world and its wickedness you must subdue the body rigorously to subject it to the spirit, and so that you can easily follow God's law. It's important at this time to take up the weapons of hairshirt, fasting, and discipline in order to eradicate the root of sin from the flesh. But when you start to progress along the road of the spirit, by undertaking interior discipline, you must moderate bodily penance, as you're sufficiently exercised by the spirit: your heart will grow weak, your chest will suffer, your brain will grow tired, and your whole body will grow heavy and clumsy for the functions of the soul.

(115) The wise and experienced guide must be careful not to allow these people to indulge in the excesses of bodily penance to which they're moved by God's grandeur in dark and purifying interior recollection. It's not good to consume body and spirit at the same time, or break your strength with harsh and excessive penances, as you will already be weakened by interior discipline. For this reason St Ignatius of Loyola said in his Exercises that bodily penances were necessary on the purgative way, but that they should be moderated in the illuminative life, and much more so in the unitive.

(116) But you will say to me that the saints used awful penances. In fact they didn't use them indiscreetly or at their own discretion, but on the advice of their spiritual director or superiors, who allowed them because they realized they were inwardly moved by God to these rigours, and to confound sinners by their example, and for many other reasons. At other times penances were permitted to dampen the ardour of the spirit and to counteract raptures, which are all special reasons and don't apply to everyone.

Chapter 16

The great difference between exterior and interior penances

(117) The penances that you apply to yourself are very light (although they may have been harsh to start with) when compared with those administered by someone else. This is because in the first instance you undertake them at your own discretion, and the more voluntary they are, the less their impact, because ultimately you do as you wish. But in the second instance they are painful, by virtue of the fact that they are given by somebody else.

(118) This is what Jesus said to St Peter: When you are young and a beginner in virtue, you discipline yourself, but when you are older and accustomed to the ways of virtue, someone else must discipline you. And then if you want to follow me, denying yourself completely, you must lay down your cross and take up mine: that is to say, allow another to crucify you (John 21:18).

(119) You mustn't differentiate: not between your father or your son, and not between your friend or your brother. These may well be the first to humble you and speak against you, for whatever reason, calling your virtue deceitful, hypocritical or foolishness, and putting obstacles in the path of your exercises. All this and much else besides will happen to you if you really want to serve God and allow yourself to be disciplined by him.

(120) Rest assured that although the disciplines and exterior penances that you apply to yourself are good, you won't achieve perfection with them alone, because although they subdue the body, they don't purify the soul or the passions, which prevent perfect contemplation and divine union.

(121) It's very easy to discipline the body by means of the spirit, but not the spirit by means of the body. In reality, it's essential with interior discipline to struggle unstintingly all your life, in order to overcome the passions and root out self-love, even though you're in an exalted state. And so you must make every effort with interior discipline, because exterior and bodily discipline is not enough, though holy and good.

(122) Although you may undergo all the suffering in the world, and undertake harsher penances than have been witnessed to this day in God's Church, if you don't deny yourself and discipline yourself inwardly, you'll be very far from achieving perfection.

(123) A good proof of this is what happened to the Blessed Henry Suso, who spent twenty years suffering rigorous hairshirts, disciplines and abstinences so great that just reading about them inspires revulsion, until God gave him light in an ecstasy, which made him realize he hadn't even made a start. And so it was that until God disciplined him with great temptations and interior distress he didn't attain perfection. You should understand clearly now the big difference between exterior and interior penances, and between interior and exterior discipline.

Chapter 17

How you should behave when you make mistakes in order to learn from themand so that you don't become anxious

(124) Whenever you make some mistake, no matter what it is, don't get worried and upset, because they're the result of our own weak nature, stained by original sin, and so inclined to evil that we have need of a special grace, like the Holy Virgin, to stay free of venial sins.

(125) If you become anxious and agitated when you fall into error, or are negligent in some way, it's a clear sign that you're still governed by secret pride. Do you imagine you won't make mistakes any more? Is it any wonder that you commit minor errors when God allows even the most saintly of people to commit them? God allows them to make some mistakes and to continue in the bad habits they had as beginners to ensure their continued humility, and to let them think they're still beginners, as they still have a beginner's faults.

(126) Stay humble, recognize how lowly you really are, and give thanks to God for having saved you from the numerous errors you might have fallen into, and still might, dominated as you are by your inclinations and appetites. What can you expect from the crumbly soil of our own nature, except weeds, thorns and thistles? It's a miracle of divine grace that we don't make innumerable mistakes by the minute. We would shock everybody if God didn't continually take us by the hand.

(127) When you commit some error the common enemy will convince you that you're not well established on the spiritual way, that you're straying from it, that you haven't really changed your ways, that you haven't made a good general confession, that you're not truly sorry, and because of all this you've lost God and are held in disgrace. And what fear, timidity, confusion, and empty thoughts the devil will inspire in you if unfortunately you sometimes repeat a venial sin! He will persuade you that you're wasting your time, that you're doing nothing, that your prayer is useless, that you don't prepare yourself as you should to receive the Eucharist, that you don't discipline

yourself every day as you promised God, that prayer and communion without prior discipline is no good. The devil will make you distrust the divine grace with all this, by highlighting your misery and making a monster out of it, giving you to understand that every day you're getting worse instead of better, when you see how you fall into so many errors.

(128) Oh blessed soul, open your eyes, and don't allow yourself to be carried away by Satan's gilded tricks, as he's out to ruin you and to make you fearful with these spurious reasons! Cut out all these thoughts and considerations, and shut the door on all these meanderings and devilish suggestions. Set aside these unfounded fears and put faintheartedness to flight, acknowledge your misery and trust in the divine mercy. And if tomorrow you fall again, as you did today, renew your trust, over and over again, in that supreme and more than infinite goodness, which is so ready to overlook our failings and to receive us as beloved children.

Chapter 18

Continuation

(129) And so whenever you fall into error, put aside groundless fears and don't waste time with needless remorse over your lapse by worrying and getting upset. You should simply acknowledge that you've been remiss and turn to God once more in loving trust, and humbly ask his forgiveness without making a fuss about it. Remain calm once you've done this, without wondering whether or not God has forgiven you, and go back to your exercises and interior prayer as if nothing had happened.

(130) Wouldn't it be foolish for someone to go out with others to joust, and having fallen in mid course to lie there bemoaning his misfortune, and wondering about the fall? They would say "Get up, man, stop wasting time and get on with it." If he gets up promptly and carries on with the joust, it's as if he hadn't fallen.

(131) If you wish to reach the high peak of perfection and interior peace, you must wield the sword of confidence in the divine goodness, day and night, and whenever you fall. You must call upon this humble and loving gift and have complete confidence in the divine goodness to cope with all the faults and defects you are prone to, whether you fall into them deliberately or not.

(132) Even though you fall frequently and are concerned about it, you should pick yourself up and not worry, because what God doesn't do in forty years he will perhaps do in an instant by a special mystery, so that we live humbled and know that it's the work of God's almighty hand to free us from faults in this way.

(133) God in his ineffable wisdom also wants us to make a stairway to heaven not only through our virtues, but also through those vices and passions with which the devil endeavours to cast us into the abyss. "Let us ascend also by our vices and passions," said St Augustine. So that we don't make poison out of medicine and vices out of virtues, and become proud of them, God prefers virtues to vices, by curing us with what harms us. This is how St Gregory puts it: "As we make a wound out of our medicine, God makes a medicine of our wound, so that we who are injured by virtue may be cured by vice."

(134) God makes us understand by means of these little falls from grace that it is he who sets us free from the big ones. In this way we're made humble and vigilant, which is what our overweening nature needs. And so although you must walk very carefully so as not to fall into any error or imperfection, if you fall once or a thousand times, you must use the remedy I've given you, which is to have loving trust in the divine mercy. This is the weapon with which you must fight and overcome faintheartedness and unprofitable fretting. This is the remedy to help you not to waste time, not to grow anxious, and to make progress. This is the treasure with which you must enrich your soul. And by these means, finally, you will reach the peak of the high mountain of perfection, tranquillity, and interior peace.

Third Book
On the spiritual disciplines with which God purifies souls, infused and passive contemplation, perfect resignation, interior humility, divine wisdom, true annihilation, and interior peace

Chapter 1

The difference between the exterior and the interior person

(1) There are two kinds of spiritual persons: those who are interior, and those who are exterior. The latter seek God by external means such as discursive reasoning, imagination, and conceptual thinking, and strive earnestly to attain virtue through great abstinence, mortification of the body and the senses. These people undertake rigorous penances, put on hairshirts, punish the flesh with various disciplines, struggle to attain silence and to induce a sense of God's presence, alternately imagining God as a shepherd, as a doctor, or as a loving lord and father. They also delight in continually talking about God, and very often give vent to fervent expressions of love for him, all of which is artificial and falls within the realm of meditation.

(2) These same people wish to feel important, and by means of voluntary and exterior mortification seek to induce emotions based on the senses, and passionate feelings, thinking that only when they have them does God dwell within them.

(3) This is the exterior way of beginners, and although it's good in itself, these people will never achieve perfection this way, or even take one step toward it, as shown by the experience of many others who after fifty years of this exterior exercise are empty of God and full of themselves, and are spiritual in name only.

(4) There are other genuinely spiritual people who have moved on from the beginnings of the interior way that leads to perfection and union with God, and to which God in his infinite compassion called

them from the exterior way they were following at the start. These recollected people who have truly surrendered themselves into God's hands with total nakedness and obliviousness, even of themselves, are always uplifted in the presence of God. They abide in God with pure faith, without image, shape or form, but with great confidence born of interior peace and tranquillity. In this state of infused recollection the spirit gathers itself with such force that it concentrates inwardly the mind, the heart, the body, and all its physical powers.

(5) Those people who have undergone interior discipline and whom God has purified in the fire of adversity with innumerable and horrific torments, all prescribed by him and in his own way, have attained self-mastery, because they've conquered and denied themselves in all things, and so live in great serenity and interior peace. And although they often feel revulsion and suffer temptation, they quickly emerge victorious, because they've been tested and imbued with divine strength, and are thus unmoved by the impulses of the passions. And although the insistent temptations and troublesome suggestions of the enemy may last for a long time, they overcome all of them to their great advantage, as God now fights for them on their behalf.

(6) These people have attained great light and a profound knowledge of Jesus Christ, both of his divinity and his humanity. They enjoy this infused knowledge in quiet silence, inwardly withdrawn in the superior part of their souls, with a spirit free from images and exterior representation, and with a love that is pure and devoid of all earthly things. They're raised up, quite beyond external activities, to a love of both humanity and divinity. They feel love for everything they deal with, and are detached from everything in which they delight, for their whole experience tells them that they love their God with all their heart and soul.

(7) These happy and exalted people delight in nothing of this world, except their own nothingness and their own solitariness, and would rather that the rest of the world left them alone, and forgot about them. They're detached to such an extent that although they continually receive supernatural favours, they remain unchanged and unaffected by them, as though they hadn't received them. At all times they preserve in their innermost heart a profound sense of their unworthiness, and remain forever in the abyss of their own abjectness and nothingness.

(8) By the same token, they remain quiet, serene, and equable, and this amidst both extraordinary graces and favours, and in the harshest and bitterest torments. There's no news that makes them happy, no event that makes them sad; adversity doesn't disturb them, and neither does the continuous, divine communication give them an inflated sense of their own worth, as they're constantly filled with holy and filial fear, and rest in wonderful peace, trust, and serenity.

Chapter 2

Continuation

(9) Those on the exterior way strive continually to practise the virtues, one after the other, in order to attain them, and endeavour to remove imperfections with laborious efforts calculated to destroy all such failings. They struggle to eradicate attachments, one by one, by different and contradictory exercises, but however much they wear themselves out they achieve nothing, because of ourselves we can do nothing that isn't miserable and imperfect.

(10) But on this interior way, in loving recollection in God's presence, virtue is established, because it's God who operates within us. Additionally, attachments are uprooted, imperfections destroyed, and the passions subdued, and so at all times these people will be free and detached without ever having thought about the good for which God in his infinite compassion has prepared them.

(11) Although such people are so advanced, blessed as they are with the true light of God, nevertheless they're deeply aware by this same light of their weakness and imperfections, and the extent to which they're deficient as regards the perfection they're aiming for. They're miserable and full of self-disgust, and have a loving fear of God, as well as self-loathing, but at the same time a genuine trust in God together with a mistrust of themselves.

(12) The more they humble themselves and have little self-regard and genuine self-knowledge, the more they please God and dwell in his presence with all respect and veneration.

(13) When they're in God's presence they set no store by all the good they do, or what they continually have to suffer, both inwardly and outwardly.

(14) They make a continual effort to enter within themselves, in God, in quiet and silence, as there they find their centre, their dwelling place, and their delight. They place a higher value on this interior withdrawal than on talking about God, and they retreat into this interior and hidden centre to meet God and to receive his divine influence with fear and loving reverence. If they leave their centre at all it's simply to admit their own nothingness.

(15) Those who attain this happy state are few in number, as there are few who are willing to acknowledge their unworthiness and to let themselves be refined and purified. For this reason, although there are many who enter on this interior way, it's rare for them to move on and not remain at the beginning. God said to one soul: "This interior way belongs to the few, or even to a very small minority. It's such a high grace that no one deserves it. It belongs to the few because this way is quite simply death to the senses, and those who are willing to die in this manner and to be annihilated are few, whereas this supreme gift depends on this very willingness."

(16) And so now you will understand and appreciate what a great difference there is between the exterior and the interior way, and how different is the presence of God born of meditation to that of the infused and supernatural presence of God that is born of infused recollection and passive contemplation. In a word, you will know what a great difference there is between the exterior and the interior person.

Chapter 3

The way to attain interior peace is not through the pleasure of the senses, or through spiritual consolation, but through the denial of self-love

(17) St Bernard said that to serve God is nothing other than to do good and suffer evil. The person who wishes to journey to perfection by way of tenderness and consolation is deceiving himself. You should want no other consolation from God than to end your life for his sake in a state of complete obedience and subjection.

(18) Christ's path was not one of softness and tenderness, and neither did he invite us to follow such a path by his example, or with these words: "If any man would come after me, let him deny himself, and take up his cross and follow me" (Matt.24:26). And so the person who wants to be joined with Christ must be like him, and follow him in suffering.

(19) You will scarcely have begun to enjoy the tenderness of divine love in prayer when the cunning enemy will urge you to seek the desert and solitude, so that without interference from anybody you can then spread your sails to receive continuous and delightful prayer.

(20) Open your eyes, and realize that these promptings are not in keeping with Christ's teaching, which didn't invite us to follow the path of tenderness and consolation, but rather the path of self-denial, saying "let him deny himself," meaning by this: "He who would follow me and attain perfection, should blind his own will totally, and forsaking everything lay himself open completely to the yoke of obedience and subjection through self-denial, which is the truest cross."

(21) Many people dedicated to God receive from him great thoughts, visions and mental ecstasies, but for all that God hasn't allowed them the gift of performing miracles, understanding hidden secrets, or foretelling the future, but God has indeed graced others who have endured adversity, temptation, and genuine hardship in a state of perfect humility, obedience, and subjection.

(22) What great good fortune it is to be in a state of subjection!

What great wealth it is to be poor! What a great honour to be lowly! How exalted it is to be cast down! What a consolation to be afflicted! What sublime knowledge to be taken for a fool! In a word, what supreme happiness to be crucified with Christ! This is the great happiness in which the Apostle gloried: "But far be it for me to glory, save in the Cross of Our Lord Jesus Christ" (Gal. 6:14). Leave it to others to glory in their wealth, status, pleasures and honours, as for us there is no other honour than to be denied, despised and crucified with Christ.

(23) But the shameful thing is that there's hardly anyone who despises spiritual pleasures and who wants to be denied for Christ's sake by embracing his Cross with love: "For many are called, but few chosen," says the Holy Spirit (Matt 22:14). Many are called to perfection, but few arrive there, because there aren't many who embrace the Cross with patience, perseverance and resignation.

(24) There are few people who deny themselves in all things, who bow to another's judgment, who continually discipline all their passions, who annihilate themselves in all respects, who always follow what's contrary to their own will, appetite and inclination. Many people teach these things, but there are few who practise them.

(25) There are many who have started out on this road, and do so every day, and who persevere while they enjoy the delightful sweetness of the honey of primitive fervour. Yet this sweetness and pleasurable taste has hardly left them when they're overtaken by the storm of adversity, temptation and aridity (all necessary to arrive at the high mountain of perfection), and then they stop and turn back on the way, which is an obvious sign that they seek themselves, and not God or perfection.

(26) May it please God that those who have seen the light and who have been called to interior peace and then turned back (because they didn't persevere in aridity, adversity and temptation), shall not be cast into outer darkness, for this would be like the person who was found without a wedding garment, and although a servant was turned away for not being properly prepared, preferring rather to be guided by his own judgment.

(27) This monster of the ego must be destroyed: the seven-headed hydra of self-love must be decapitated if we are to reach the peak of the high mountain of peace, for it's a monster that feeds on everything. Sometimes it finds its way into our conversation with relatives, conversation which we find easy and which can be strangely destructive. At other times it will insinuate itself in our dealings with the confessor in the guise of gratitude, or passionate and unrestrained

affection. Yet again you will find it in a tendency to subtle spiritual pride, or in a fondness for precious little worldly honours that mean a great deal to you. And then again it will batten onto your spiritual pleasures, and even feed on the gifts of God themselves, and on his freely bestowed graces. And yet again it will express itself as an excessive concern for your health, concealing itself as a wish for good treatment and personal comfort. Sometimes it will merely wish to appear good, but by very subtle means. And finally, it is notorious for attaching itself to your own judgment and opinion in everything, judgment and opinion whose roots are enmeshed in self-will. All these are the effects of self-love, and if it's not denied it will be impossible for you to ascend to the heights of contemplation, to the supreme happiness of loving union, and to the sublime throne of interior peace.

Chapter 4

On two spiritual disciplines with which God purifies you when he wants to unite you with him

(28) We shall now discuss how God usually uses two means to purify those he wishes to enlighten and perfect in order to unite them intimately with himself. The first way, which we shall deal with in this and the following chapter, is with the bitter waters of distress, temptations, anguish, afflictions and interior torments.

(29) The second way is with the burning fire of inflamed love, a love that is both impatient and hungry. It may be that God uses both means in those he wishes to fill with his grace, love, light and interior peace. At one time God will place them in the strong lye of tribulation and interior and exterior bitterness, burning them with the fire of severe temptation. At other times he will put them in the crucible of eager and anxious love, testing them with extreme harshness, for the more God wants union and enlightenment in a person, then the greater must be the torment and purification, because all knowledge of God and union with him is born of suffering, the true test of love.

(30) If only you could understand the enormous benefits of suffering! It's this that erases sins, purifies you, and produces patience. It's suffering in prayer that actually promotes patience, that deepens it, and enables you to perform the highest acts of charity. It's suffering that brings you joy, that draws you to God, that allows you to be called and to enter heaven. It's this that tests the true servants of God, that makes them wise, strong and constant. It's suffering, too, that disposes God more readily to hear you: "When I was in trouble I called upon the Lord: and he heard me" (Ps.119). It's suffering that annihilates, refines, and perfects. It's suffering, in a word, that makes earthly souls heavenly, and human souls divine, transforming them and uniting them wonderfully with God's humanity and divinity. St Augustine put this well when he said that our life on earth is one of temptation.

(31) Blessed is the person who suffers temptation, if he stays firm in his temptation, for temptation is the method chosen by God to humble

you, annihilate you, test you, discipline you, deny you, perfect you, and fill you with his divine gifts. By means of temptation and suffering God comes to crown and transform you. Rest assured that temptation and conflict are necessary for your perfection.

(32) Oh, blessed soul, if only you knew how to stay constant and quiet in the fire of tribulation, and let yourself be washed in the bitter waters of affliction, how soon you would find yourself rich in heavenly gifts, and how soon the divine goodness would establish in you a rich throne and beautiful dwelling place in which to find solace!

(33) God reposes only in quiet souls, where the fire of suffering and temptation has burnt away the dross of the passions, and where the bitter waters of affliction have washed away the dirty stains of disordered appetite. In short, God rests only where serenity reigns and self-love has been banished.

(34) But you will never arrive at this happy state, or experience the precious gift of interior peace, even though you manage with divine grace to overcome the exterior senses, while you remain unpurified of the disordered passions of lust, of self-love, and of your worries and desires (even if they're spiritual in nature) and of many other attachments and hidden vices that are within you, which to your intense regret will prevent the serene indwelling of God, who wishes to be united with you, and to transform himself in you.

(35) Additionally, if the very virtues you have acquired remain unpurified, then they, too, will prevent you from receiving this great gift of peace. And you will also be frustrated in your advance by any inordinate desire for sublime gifts, by your appetite for spiritual consolation, and by your attachment to infused and divine graces, as long as you delight in them and yearn to enjoy more of them. In a word, your progress will be arrested by any desire for self-gratification.

(36) How much there is to purify in the person who is to reach the holy mountain of perfection and transformation in God! How well prepared, naked, denied, and annihilated a person must be to allow God's presence and his continual communication!

(37) Divine wisdom is of the utmost importance to prepare the depths of your soul for the divine indwelling. If a seraphim is insufficient to purify you, how can you bring about your own purification – frail, wretched and inexperienced as you are?

(38) It's for this reason that God himself will make you ready and prepare you passively in the fire of tribulation and interior torment, without any intervention on your part, and without any other requirement than your willingness to bear the Cross, both inwardly and outwardly.

(39) You will experience within yourself passive aridity, darkness, anguish, conflict, continual revulsion, interior helplessness, excruciating desolation of spirit, the continual and inopportune suggestions and insistent temptations of the enemy. And finally, you will be so fraught and anguished that you will be quite unable to lift up your heart, or even make the smallest act of faith, hope, or love.

(40) In this state you will feel abandoned and prey to the passions of anger, rage, blasphemy and disordered appetites; you will feel the most miserable creature on earth, the greatest sinner, the most despised of God, and devoid of all virtue; you will suffer infernal torment when you find yourself so desolate and afflicted in this way. And you will feel utterly bereft of God, an agony that is the cruelest cross of all.

(41) But although you feel so oppressed, so full of arrogance, impatience and rage, yet these temptations shall not prevail, for the hidden virtue and strength that dwell within your most intimate depths will overcome them.

(42) Be firm, oh blessed soul, be firm, for you will never love more intensely, nor ever be nearer to God, than when you're so forlorn. For although the sun may be hidden by the clouds it doesn't vary its position or lose its magnificent splendour on that account. God allows this agonizing abandonment to cleanse and purify you, to deny you and to strip you. In this way you will be entirely given over to him, just as his infinite goodness is given entirely to you, that he may delight in you, for although you may cry and lament, God is joyful and glad in the most secret and hidden depths of your soul.

Chapter 5

How important and necessary it is to suffer unstintingly this first spiritual torment

(43) For your earthly soul to become heavenly, and for you to reach the Highest Good, which is union with God, you must be purified in the fire of tribulation and temptation.

(44) Although it's a truism that all those who serve God must suffer troubles, problems, and distress, those fortunate people who are guided by God along the hidden and interior way of purifying contemplation must above all suffer harsh and terrible temptations and atrocious torment in greater measure than did those whom the primitive Church revered as martyrs.

(45) The martyrs, apart from the brevity of their suffering, which barely lasted days, were able to comfort themselves with the clear light and the expectation of imminent and sure reward. On the other hand, those abandoned must die to self and be stripped and cleansed, experience the loss of God, temptation, darkness, anguish, grief, harsh and rigorous aridities, and endure death at each instant through painful torment and tremendous desolation. And neither do they receive the slightest consolation: on the contrary, their affliction is so intense that their agony is nothing short of a protracted death and continuous martyrdom. But the pity of it is that those who follow Christ in peace and resignation in such distress are few and far between.

(46) Formerly, people were martyred and God gave them comfort. In this case it's God who afflicts them, by hiding himself, while the demons like cruel executioners torment body and soul in a thousand ways, and the whole person is crucified both inwardly and outwardly.

(47) Your anguish will appear insuperable, your troubles inconsolable, and it will seem that heaven no longer bestows its blessings upon you. You will feel beside yourself with grief, hemmed in by inward torment and the darkness of your faculties, and frustrated by the powerlessness of prayer; you will be assailed by insistent temptations, painful uncertainty, and nagging scruples; light and judgment itself will desert you.

(48) All things on earth will trouble you; spiritual advice will distress you; the reading of books, no matter how holy, will not comfort you as they used to; if you're advised to be patient, then this will annoy you intensely; the fear of losing God because of your ingratitude and lack of response will worry you enormously. If you cry out and beg for God's help, instead of relief you will feel inward reproach and distress, like another Caananite woman to whom God at first gave no answer and then treated like a dog.

(49) Although God won't desert you at this time because it would be impossible to exist for an instant without his help, nevertheless, his support will be so hidden that you will be unaware of it, and neither will you be capable of receiving hope or consolation. On the contrary, you will think you're irredeemable and suffering like those condemned to the pains of hell, pains which you would willingly exchange for a violent death and be very glad of it, but just like those condemned, an end to your afflictions and bitterness will seem impossible to you – "The pains of death compassed me round about: and the pains of hell got hold upon me" (Ps. 114).

(50) But, oh blessed soul, if only you knew how much you were beloved and supported by God in the midst of these torments, then you would find them so sweet that God would have to perform a miracle to let you live. Be firm, oh happy soul, be firm, and be of good courage, for although you feel unbearable in this state, you will be well protected by the Highest Good, and moreover loved and enriched, as if God had no other thought in mind than to lead you to perfection through the exaltation of love.

(51) And if you don't turn back, but persist with courage, without giving up on your task, then you will make the most admirable sacrifice to God, so that if God were capable of pain he would never rest until union with him was secured.

(52) And if almighty God has worked so many miracles in the chaos of the Void, then what will he do for you who are made in his own image and likeness, if you persevere with courage, quiet and resigned, and with a true knowledge of your own nothingness? Happy indeed is the person who though troubled, afflicted and desolate, remains constant within and doesn't venture forth to seek the exterior consolation.

(53) Don't worry and fret too much if these excruciating torments continue: persevere with humility and don't seek support from outside sources, for your spiritual welfare consists in silence, suffering, quiet patience and resignation, and here you will find the divine fortress to fight for you in such a bitter war. He who fights on your behalf is within yourself, for God is that fortress.

(54) When you're immersed in this painful state of utter desolation, weeping and complaining are permissible, so long as you remain resigned in the higher part of your soul, for who could suffer the heavy hand of God without tears? Job, that great servant of God, himself lamented, and even Christ wept in his abandonment, although both of them remained resigned.

(55) Don't be alarmed when God crucifies you and tests your loyalty: follow the example of the woman of Caanan who when rejected by God nevertheless humbled herself and followed him, even though God treated her like a dog. You must drink from the chalice, and not turn back. If like St Paul the scales are removed from your eyes, then you would see the importance of suffering and glory in it like him, who thought more highly of being crucified than of being an apostle.

(56) Happiness doesn't lie in pleasure but in suffering. St Teresa appeared to someone after her death and told her that she'd been rewarded only for her suffering and that she hadn't been rewarded one iota for all the ecstasies, revelations and consolations that she'd enjoyed in this life.

(57) Although the torments of passive purification and the resulting alienation from God are so awful that the mystics rightly call it hell (because it seems impossible to survive such atrocious distress for a moment, so you might really say that the person who suffers it endures a living death, and those dying suffer a lingering death), nevertheless you must suffer this to attain the sweet, gentle, and abundant blessing of advanced contemplation and loving union. And there has never been a saint who has reached this state who hasn't passed through this spiritual distress and painful torment. St Gregory went through it in the last two months of his life, while St Francis of Assisi endured two and a half years of it. St Mary Magdalen of Pazzi suffered five years in this condition, while St Rose of Lima underwent fifteen years of purification. And after performing so many miracles to everybody's amazement St Dominic suffered until half an hour before his happy demise. And so if you want to become like the saints, you must suffer as they did.

Chapter 6

On the second spiritual torment with which God purifies you when he wants to unite you with him

(58) The other torment, which is more meritorious and beneficial for those proficient in deep contemplation and the spiritual life, is the fire of divine love that burns the soul and will cause you to suffer from this very love. Sometimes the absence of your beloved God will trouble you; at other times the soft, gentle, burning intensity of God's presence will torment you, an intensity that's so sweet that it will make you yearn for him always. Sometimes when you possess and delight in your beloved God you will hardly be able to contain yourself with the sheer joy of possession; at other times, when God doesn't reveal himself to you, then you will long with a burning anxiety to go in search of him, to find him, and to delight in him, at which point the yearning, suffering, and dying from love will be excruciatingly intense to you.

(59) If only you could understand the paradoxes that beset the one who loves – a conflict that's so terrible and bitter on the one hand, so sweet, gentle and loving on the other! At times the pain with which love torments you will be sharp and penetrating, and at other times your suffering will be so bitter-sweet that you wouldn't wish to exchange it for anything in the world.

(60) As light and love increase so does your grief for the absence of the one whom you love so keenly. To feel the nearness of such good is joy, and the powerlessness to embrace it perfectly is death in life. Although you have food and drink to hand, and you may be hungry and thirsty, you will not be satisfied; you will be immersed and engulfed in an ocean of love with the powerful hand nearby that can help you, and which fails to do so; and neither do you know when you will ever see the one whom you desire so intensely.

(61) At times you will hear the interior voice of your beloved God telling you to hasten to him, or you will hear a gentle whisper that proceeds from the innermost depths of your being where God resides,

and which will penetrate you vigorously until you dissolve and melt away, as you then become aware of God's intimacy within you, and at the same time how far away he is when you fail to possess him. This experience will intoxicate you, will make you faint, will overwhelm you, and will fill you with insatiable desire, which is why love is likened to death, for like death it also kills.

Chapter 7

Interior discipline and perfect resignation are necessary to attain interior peace

(62) The subtlest arrow that nature fires in our direction is the one that seduces us to indulge in what is illicit on the pretext that it's necessary and beneficial. How many have allowed themselves to be carried away and become lost through this gilded deceit! You will never taste the delightful manna, (which no-one knoweth but he that receiveth it: Rev.) if you don't exercise perfect self-control, to the extent that you die to yourself, for the person who doesn't strive to die to his passions is not ready to receive the gift of insight without whose inspiration it will be impossible for you to turn inward and for your spirit to be transformed. And so those who are unable to enter within themselves must live without this gift.

(63) Resign yourself and deny yourself in all things, for although true self-denial is difficult to start with, it's easier as you get on, and is very pleasant by the end. You will know that you're very far from perfection if you don't see God in everything. Pure, perfect and essential love consists in the Cross, in voluntary self-denial, in perfect humility, poverty of spirit, and a low regard for your own importance.

(64) During the time of strong temptation, abandonment and desolation, it's important to enter within yourself and to remain in your innermost centre, so that you contemplate and gaze upon God who has his throne and his quiet in your most inward being. Otherwise you will experience impatience and bitterness of heart born of a love that is empty, ill-disciplined, and deriving from the senses. You will know true love and its effects when you feel truly humble, sincerely desire to be self-disciplined, and have a profound sense of your own insignificance.

(65) There are many people who dedicate themselves to prayer who don't experience God because when they leave prayer they take no further trouble to discipline themselves or even think about God. To attain a serene and continuous gaze upon God you must have great purity of heart and mind, great peace in your soul, and total resignation.

(66) Our happiness resides in our innermost being where God

reveals to us his miracles. Here we are immersed and lose ourselves in the immense ocean of God's infinite goodness, where we remain steadfast and immovable, and where we encounter the ineffable fulfilment of our soul, and supreme, loving quiet. The humble and resigned person who establishes himself in this centre seeks only to fulfil God's will, a will whose divine and loving spirit imparts a knowledge of all things with a gentle yet vigorous warmth.

(67) There are some giants among the saints who continually suffer with patience the weaknesses of the flesh, about which God cares a great deal. But the supreme gift belongs to those who through the strength of the Holy Spirit bear inward and outward distress with patience and resignation. This kind of sanctity is as rare as it is precious in the eyes of God. Those spiritual persons who travel this road are few in number, for there are few in this world who totally deny themselves, to follow Christ crucified with sincerity and nakedness of spirit along the thorny and deserted ways of the Cross, without taking thought for themselves.

(68) The life of self-denial surpasses all the miracles of the saints. Those who lead such a life will be unaware whether or not they live or die, are lost or found, whether they consent or not, for they're incapable of reflecting on anything: this is the life of the truly resigned. But although you may not reach this state for a very long time, don't despair, for God can give you in an instant what you have been denied for many years until then.

(69) Those who are willing to suffer blindly without consolation from God or man are well able to bear unjust accusations from their enemies, even when they're undergoing the most tremendous interior desolation.

(70) Spiritual persons who live for God and in God, in the midst of bodily and spiritual torment, are inwardly content, for adversity and the Cross are their life and their delight. Tribulation is the great treasure with which God honours those who follow him in this life. For this reason wicked people are necessary to those who are good, as too is the devil who so troubles us by seeking our ruination, but who actually does us the greatest service imaginable. To be of any value to God human life and suffering must be inseparable, just as the body and soul are, or the soul and grace, and the earth and the sun. On the threshing-floor of the soul God separates the wheat from the chaff with the wind of tribulation.

(71) When God crucifies you in your most intimate depths, nobody will be able to console you – on the contrary, consolation itself will be a bitter cross to bear. And if you're well versed in the rules and

disciplines of the way of pure love, then you will be unable to seek outside consolation and support when you're undergoing inward trials and desolation – and neither must you try. You will also be unable to read spiritual books, for this is a devious way of avoiding suffering.

(72) Take pity on those who can't be persuaded that suffering and adversity are of the greatest benefit. Even those who have attained perfection must always be willing to suffer and to die to themselves. Those who don't suffer are empty, for we were born to work and to suffer, and those who are the friends and elect of God, even more so.

(73) Rest assured that to attain total transformation in God you must lose yourself and deny your life, feelings, understanding and power, and be living yet not living, dying yet not dying, suffering yet not suffering, resigned, yet not resigned – in fact, making no logical connections at all.

(74) The seekers after perfection become great only through fire, distress, grief, torment, afflictions, and self-abasement willingly accepted. And the person who is always looking for somewhere to rest his head and not transcend the realm of reason and the senses shall never enter the hidden retreat of mystical knowledge, although he may enjoy reading about it and have an intellectual grasp of the subject.

Chapter 8

Continuation

(75) God will never reveal himself to you so long as you haven't died to yourself in both your senses and faculties. You will never reach this state until you're perfectly resigned and determined to be with God alone, valuing equally his gifts as well as contempt, light as well as darkness, and peace as well as war. And so to attain perfect quiet and supreme interior peace you must first die to yourself and live only in God and for God.

(76) The more you die to yourself, the more you will know God. But if you don't concentrate on continual self-denial and inward discipline you will never achieve this state, or preserve God within you. On the contrary, you will always be subject to the accidents and passions of the spirit, such as judging people, gossiping, resentment, making excuses, and defending yourself to maintain your honour and self-esteem, all of which are enemies of quiet, perfection, peace, and the spirit.

(77) The difference between spiritual people consists only in the extent to which they die to themselves, for God has his paradise, his honour, his blessings, and his delight on earth in those who die to themselves continually. The difference between doing, suffering, and dying, is great: doing is pleasant and for beginners; willing suffering is characteristic of proficients; and always dying to oneself is the mark of proficients and the perfect, of whom there are very few in this world.

(78) How happy you will be if your only concern is to die to yourself, for then you will not only gain victory over your enemies, but also over yourself, a victory in which you will surely find pure love, perfect quiet, and divine wisdom. It's impossible to live and think mystically, with a simple understanding of divine and infused wisdom, if we don't first die to ourselves through the absolute negation of our senses and reasoning powers.

(79) The real lesson for spiritual persons, and one that you must learn, is to leave well alone and not involve yourself or interfere in

anything that is not your responsibility, for those who train themselves to leave everything to God then begin to possess everything for eternity.

(80) There are some people who seek rest; others, without looking for it, experience rest; some experience pain, while others seek it out. The first don't progress at all; the second walk in the right direction; the third run, and the last fly.

(81) To devalue pleasure and to consider it a torment is the mark of a truly self-disciplined person. Interior peace and joy are the fruits of the divine spirit, and none receive them if they're not fully resigned in their heart. Good people's annoyance soon passes, but nevertheless they try not to succumb to it, for anger damages the health, disturbs the spirit, and causes anxiety.

(82) Among other good advice you should follow, remember this: don't dwell on the faults of others but look to your own, preserve a constant and prayerful interior silence and deny yourself in everything and at all times, for in this way you will guard against many faults and become master of many virtues. Never think ill of anybody, for unwarranted suspicion of others disturbs the purity of your heart, makes you anxious, draws you away from your centre, and unsettles you.

(83) You will never achieve perfect resignation if you actively seek the respect of others and allow yourself to be flattered by what they say about you. If those on the interior way rely solely on reason in their dealings with the world they will come adrift; the most reasonable approach is to disregard reason altogether and to accept that God permits injustice to befall us in order to humble us and to annihilate our self-will, so that we live resigned in everything. You must realize that God thinks more highly of those who are inwardly resigned than those who perform miracles, even if they can raise the dead.

(84) There are some people who practise prayer but who don't have interior discipline and therefore always remain full of faults and self-love. It's a truism that nobody can hurt those who think little of themselves and who are aware of their own insignificance. Finally, hope, suffer, be silent, and have patience: let nothing upset you or make you afraid, for all things come to an end. Only God is unchangeable, and patience will obtain everything. The person who has God, has everything; the person who doesn't have God, has nothing (St Teresa).

Chapter 9

To attain interior peace you must accept
your own insignificance

(85) If you don't fall into error you will never fully realize your own insignificance, even though you listen to what others say about you and read spiritual books. You will never attain to precious peace if you don't first recognize your wretched frailty. Where there is no clear idea of failings then any remedy will be difficult.

(86) God will allow you some failing or other, for with this self-knowledge, when you see yourself falling into error so often, you will come to realize your own nothingness, a realization that is the basis for true humility and true peace. And so that you may better understand your weaknesses and who you really are, I want to draw your attention to some of your many faults.

(87) Sometimes you can be so full of yourself that if in the normal course of events you're frustrated, or your way forward is blocked, then you feel dreadful. Or if you're denied your rights, or someone displeases you, then you become livid with resentment. It may be that you notice a fault in someone else and instead of feeling sorry for him and admitting that you're prone to the same failing, you reproach him unnecessarily. At other times you may hanker after something to make life easier and you can't have it, and then you become embittered and depressed. At other times you may be slighted by someone and complain and get upset. And in this way you allow any kind of childishness to ruffle and upset you both inwardly and in external matters.

(88) You might well want to exercise patience, so long as it's someone else's patience. And if you're continually impatient you will try your hardest to blame someone else, without noticing that you yourself are insufferable. And when you've got over your annoyance you cunningly try to appear virtuous again, spouting moral precepts and spiritual references with all the subtlety you can muster, but without remedying your own defects. Even though you may willingly admit your faults in front of others, this has more to do with putting yourself right in their eyes than any sincere wish on your part to be really humble.

(89) At still other times you will subtly assert that you're taking someone else to task out of a sense of justice and not through any fault of your own. You might also persuade yourself that for the most part you're virtuous, steadfast and brave, to the point of giving your life up to a tyrant, solely for the love of God yet as soon as you're the victim of some spiteful little remark, you get anxious and upset. All of this is the manipulation of your own ego and your own secret pride, which should make you realize that you're dominated by love of self, which is the greatest barrier to precious peace.

Chapter 10

Descriptions of true and false humility and their effects

(90) There are two kinds of humility, one false and the other genuine. False humility belongs to those people who are like water that must rise and who take an apparent fall and make a show of repentance to get back up again. These people avoid honour and esteem to be seen as humble; they say of themselves that they're wicked so that others will think they're virtuous, and although they're aware of their wretchedness, they don't want other people to know about it. This is false humility and secret pride.

(91) Those who aspire to perfection discipline their passions; having done this, they deny themselves; then, with divine assistance, they enter the Void, where the ego has no place, self-will is set at naught, and they reach a state of awareness where they realize that of themselves they are nothing, that they can do nothing, and that they are worth nothing. From this position they die to senses and self, in many ways and at all times; and finally, from this spiritual death arises true and perfect annihilation. And so, when you're dead to your desires and understanding you may justifiably be said to have arrived at a perfect state of joyous annihilation without any awareness on your part, for you would not be annihilated if you were conscious of the fact. And although you've attained this happy state of annihilation, it's important to remember that you've yet more distance to travel, more to purify, and more to annihilate.

((92) A genuine knowledge of true, inward humility doesn't consist of outward actions, in accepting a lowly status, in dressing poorly, speaking submissively, closing your eyes, sighing affectionately, or accusing yourself of faults by saying you're worthless in order to make others think you're humble. It consists simply of having a low regard for your own importance and in a desire for self-abasement, a desire that proceeds from a profound self-knowledge, and an insouciance with respect to your humility, even though an angel draws your attention to it.

(93) The river of light with which God in his grace illumines you

does two things: it reveals the grandeur of God himself and at the same time acquaints you with the stench of your own nothingness, to such an extent that there's no language to describe the abyss in which you find yourself submerged and the pressing need you feel to let everyone know how vile you are. But the more you recognize that it's solely God's goodness and compassion that liberates you, the further removed from arrogance and conceit you will be.

(94) You will never be harmed by man or the devil, only by yourself and your own pride and the violence of your passions. Watch yourself, for you yourself are the worst devil from hell. It's hardly right that you should think about your reputation when Christ himself was considered a fool, a drunkard, and a man possessed. Oh, the folly of us Christians, that we should want to enjoy happiness without wanting to imitate him on the Cross or to share in his ignominy, his humanity, his poverty and other virtues!

(95) Truly humble people rest in the quietness of their heart, and here they are tested by God, by man and the devil, beyond all reason and discretion, yet remain self-possessed in peace and quiet. They desire in all humility to please God, in life as in death. External matters don't make them at all anxious: it's as though they didn't exist, for they delight only in death and the Cross, though they give no outward sign of it. But alas, who are these people, for there are so few of these humble souls in the world?

(96) You must hope, desire, suffer, and die unknown, for in this way you show humble and perfect love. What peace you will experience if you're profoundly humble and abase yourself! You will never be perfectly humble if when you're aware of your wretchedness you don't display this awareness to others, for then you will avoid praise, accept insult, have a low regard for all worldly things, including yourself, and if adversity befalls you, you won't blame anyone but accept it from God, the giver of all good.

(97) If you want to tolerate the failings of others, first look at your own. And if you think that you've made some progress in perfection by yourself then you're not humble at all, or have even taken one step on the spiritual way.

(98) True humility is as low as your body in the grave: your ego should be buried for dead, for it's stinking and corrupt, dust and nothingness. And so if you wish to be happy learn to have a low opinion of yourself, and to be despised by others.

Chapter 11

Maxims by which to know the simple, humble and genuine heart

(99) Take courage and humble yourself by accepting adversity as the means to your well-being. Rejoice in the contempt of others and want God alone for your refuge, protection and consolation. None, however important they are in this life, are more honoured than they deserve to be in the eyes of God, and so truly humble people set little store by this world, including themselves, and their only repose and rest is in God.

(100) Truly humble people suffer inward distress quietly and patiently and so travel a great distance in a short time, like a navigator who sails before the wind.

(101) Truly humble people see God in all things, and so everything that the world offers by way of contempt, insult, and affront they receive with great peace and interior quiet as though these disparagements were sent to them by God himself, thereby showing their great love for the means that God uses to test them.

(102) Those who are pleased by praise have not attained genuine humility, even though they don't want it or look for it, because praise is a bitter cross to those humble of heart, provided they remain quiet and immovable in all things.

(103) Those who don't have a mortal hatred of their own ego, even though they're quiet and serene, haven't acquired inward humility. But they will never possess this treasure if they don't have a profound awareness of their own misery and wretchedness.

(104) Those who take refuge in excuses and retaliation don't have a heart that's simple and humble, especially if they do these things with their superiors, because retaliation is born of secret pride that reigns in the soul, which leads to absolute ruin.

(105) Stubbornness implies a lack of submission and hence of humility, and both encourage anxiety, discord, and unrest.

(106) Humble people don't become anxious because of their failings though they pierce them to the quick, purely because they're contrary to their loving God. Neither are they bothered if they're unable to do great things in life, because they always rest in the Void and their

own nothingness. On the contrary, they're amazed when they manage to do something worthwhile, for they then thank God in the knowledge that it's God who does everything for them, and so they're always dissatisfied with what they do themselves.

(107) Truly humble people pronounce judgment on nothing, even if they see through everything, because they judge ill only of themselves.

(108) Truly humble people always find an excuse to defend anyone who hurts them, at least when the hurt is well-intentioned. After all, who can be annoyed with someone who's well-intentioned?

(109) False humility displeases God as much as true pride – in fact more so, for the former is also hypocrisy.

(110) Truly humble people don't get upset and anxious when things go wrong for them, because they're prepared for this and believe they deserve even less for themselves. They're unconcerned about the troublesome thoughts with which the devil torments them, as they're unconcerned about temptation, adversity and desolation – rather, they feel themselves to be unworthy and find great comfort in the fact that God torments them through the devil, evil though he is, and shrug off all their suffering, and neither do they ever do anything they consider worth making a fuss about.

(111) Those who have attained perfect interior humility don't get anxious about anything because they despise themselves for their failings, ingratitude, and wretchedness, all of which cause them a great deal of heartache. This is the sign by which you know the sincerely humble of heart. But the happy beings who have such a holy hatred of their own ego live immersed in the depths of the Void from where God raises them up to infuse his divine wisdom, thereby filling them with light, peace, tranquillity, and love.

Chapter 12

Interior solitude is the chief means of attaining interior peace

(112) Although solitude in itself is a great help in attaining interior peace, God wasn't speaking of this when he said through his prophet: "I will bring her into the wilderness, and speak comfortably unto her" (Hos.2:14). Rather God was referring to interior solitude, which is the only solitude that leads to the precious pearl of interior peace. Interior solitude consists in obliviousness of all external things, in detachment and perfect abnegation of all emotions, desires, thoughts and self-will. This is true solitude, where the soul rests with a loving and intimate serenity in the arms of the Highest Good.

(113) Oh, what infinite distances there are in the soul that has attained this divine solitude! Oh, what inward, withdrawn, secret, immense, and vast ranges there are within the happy soul that is truly solitary! There God communes and converses inwardly with you. There God fills you with himself, because you are empty; God clothes you with his light and love, because you are naked; God exalts you, because you are lowly; God unites you with himself and transforms you, because you are alone.

(114) Oh, gentle solitude, symbol of eternal bliss! Oh, mirror of the soul, in which the eternal Father is forever reflected! With reason you are called solitude, for you are so alone that there is scarcely a soul that seeks you out, that knows you and loves you. Oh, my Lord! How can it be that earthly souls do not aspire to this glory? How can they lose so great a good by their love and desire for created things! Blessed soul, how happy you will be if you leave all to God's care! Search out God alone, yearn for him alone, sigh for him alone. Desire nothing, and nothing will cause you disquiet, and if you do endeavour to do good, however spiritual it is, may you not be distressed if you do not succeed.

(115) If you freely give to God a soul that is detached, free, and alone, you will be the happiest creature on earth, for in this sacred solitude the Almighty has his secret dwelling place. In this desert and paradise God communes with you, and only in this interior retreat can

you hear the wonderful, powerful, interior and divine voice. If you wish to enter this heaven on earth, put aside all thought and care, and empty yourself that God's love may fill your soul. Live entirely abstracted from all created beings, surrender yourself totally to your creator, and offer yourself as sacrifice in peace and tranquillity of spirit.

(116) The more naked you are, the better you can penetrate this interior solitude and become clothed with God; the more you remain alone and empty of yourself, the more you will be filled with the divine spirit.

(117) There is no life more blissful than the life of solitude, for in this happy state God gives himself entirely to his creature, and the creature to God, in an intimate and gentle union of love. Oh, how few there are who delight in this true solitude! Truly to enjoy it you must forsake all creatures and be unmindful of yourself, for otherwise you will not become united inwardly with God.

(118) There are many who forsake all the things of this world but who fail to relinquish their own appetite, self-will, and themselves, and so there are very few who dwell in true solitude. If you are not detached from appetite, desire, self-will, and the need to delight in the spiritual gifts themselves, you will not attain the supreme happiness of interior solitude.

(119) Press on, oh blessed soul, press on without pause to this bliss of interior solitude. Pay heed to how God calls you to enter your innermost centre, where he will restore you, change you, satisfy you, clothe you, and show you a new and heavenly kingdom full of joy, peace, contentment and serenity.

Chapter 13

An explanation of infused and passive contemplation and its wonderful effects

(120) When you're practised in the interior recollection and acquired contemplation we've described; when you're purified and willing to deny your appetites at all times; when you truly exercise self-denial, and wish with all your heart to die to your passions and self-will, then God will draw you to him, raising you without your realizing it to a perfect serenity, gently and intimately infusing you with his light, his love and his strength, filling you with his warmth and an ardent desire to live a life of complete integrity.

(121) At this point also God suspends your natural faculties, and lulls you into the softest and gentlest sleep. Calm and serene in this state you will receive and enjoy, without being aware of it, the softest and gentlest equanimity of spirit. Rapt and exalted in this passive state you will be united to the Highest Good, without any effort on your part. And at this highest point and sacred temple of your heart God will delight to dwell, to reveal himself to you, and give himself over to you, God's creature, transcending your senses and all your human understanding. There also, this one pure spirit, which is God, will reign supreme over the purity of a soul now incapable of comprehending the things of the senses, filling you with complete enlightenment and the knowledge necessary for the purest and most perfect union with him.

(122) Returning to yourself from this divine embrace you will be transfused with light, love and a reverence for the divine grandeur and an awareness of your own abjectness, being now divinely altered and encouraged to suffer, to endure, and to live a life that is completely blameless.

(123) This pure, simple, infused and passive contemplation, then, is an actual and intimate revelation of God himself, of his peace and gentleness: God unalloyed, pure, ineffable, stripped of all thought in interior silence. But it's God who delights us, God who draws us to him, God who exalts us simply and spiritually: an admirable gift God grants to whomsoever he pleases, as he pleases, whenever he pleases, and for as long as he pleases, even though this state of being has more in common with the Cross, with patience, humility and suffering, than

hear the soft interior and inspirational voice of God in the midst of the tumult and turmoil of the senses? And how can you possibly be aware of this pure, heavenly spirit amid the artificialities of reason and reflection? If you are unwilling continually to die to yourself by rejecting support from the senses, then your contemplation will be pure vanity, an empty arrogance and complacency.

Chapter 14

Continuation

(125) God doesn't always communicate himself with equal abundance in the gentleness of infused contemplation. God grants this grace at some times more than others and perhaps doesn't always wait until you're fully annihilated and dead to yourself, for as this gift is pure grace on his part he gives it whenever he pleases, to whomever he pleases, and as he pleases, without there being a general rule in the matter, or any limit to his divine largesse. On the other hand, by virtue of this same contemplation, God will cause you to deny yourself, to annihilate yourself, and to die to yourself.

(126) In this state God will perhaps sometimes give more light to the understanding, and at other times perhaps greater love to the will. There's no need here for you to exhaust yourself, for all you have to do is to be receptive to whatever God gives you and rest united with him so that he may do with you as he pleases. God is Lord, and as he lays you to sleep, so will he fill you and possess you, and work powerfully and gently within you, without any effort on your part, and without your being aware of his activity. So that before you become awakened to such immense compassion you will find yourself possessed, won over, and divinely altered.

(127) The person who is in this blissful state must guard against two things: attachment, and the activity of the human spirit, for we're loath to die to ourselves, but love to be active and to use our reason in our own way, delighting in its activities. What's required at this time is great trust and nakedness of spirit to benefit from this perfect, passive capacity for receiving the divine influences, for your habitual inclination to use your mind freely and actively is a hindrance to your annihilation in God.

(128) The second pitfall is attachment to contemplation itself, and so you must strive for complete renunciation, even of God, without seeking either inwardly or externally any other goal than his divine will.

(129) In a word, you must for your part prepare yourself for this purely passive prayer by total and absolute surrender into God's hands

with perfect submission to his most holy will, so that you're occupied solely according to his pleasure, receiving with equanimity and perfect resignation whatever he may ordain.

(130) There are few people who achieve this infused and passive prayer because there are few capable of receiving God's divine influences with total nakedness of spirit and annihilation of their own activity and powers. Only those people who experience these influences will understand that this perfect detachment is only achievable with divine grace and with continual, inward mortification, and a dying to all one's inclinations and desires.

(131) Under no circumstances should you dwell upon the effects that contemplation produces within you, and especially at this time, because to do so will hinder God's activity that enriches you. You should only wish to be indifferent to your condition and remain resigned and oblivious, without awareness of God who will then prepare you for the practice of virtue, a true love of the Cross, your own nothingness, and self-annihilation, for only such total renunciation will produce a compelling desire for total perfection and the purest and most loving union.

Chapter 15

On two ways of attaining infused contemplation, and an explanation of what the stages are, and how many

(132) There are two ways to attain the joy of contemplation and perfect love: by pleasure, and through desire. At first God usually fills you with the pleasures of the senses, because you're so frail and miserable that without this prior consolation you can't possibly achieve fulfilment in heavenly things. In this first stage you prepare yourself in contrition and practise repentance by meditating on Christ's Passion, and in this way you diligently uproot worldly desires and bad habits, for the kingdom of heaven itself suffers violence and can't be conquered by the weak and timid but only by those who are very strict with themselves.

(133) The second way is through desire. The more you delight in heavenly things, the more you yearn for them, and so, having once experienced spiritual pleasures, the desire to experience divine bliss and to despise worldly pleasures is the natural outcome. From this desire is born the inclination to imitate Jesus, who said: "I am the way" (John 14: 6). The various qualities required for these stages of the imitation of Christ are as follows: humility, meekness, patience, poverty of spirit, disdain for the ego, love of the Cross, prayer and self-mortification.

(134) There are three stages in infused contemplation and the first stage is that of total fulfilment. When you're filled with God then you conceive a hatred for all worldly things and you will be serene and content with nothing less than the love of God. The second stage is that of spiritual inebriation when you will experience rapture and spiritual ecstasy born of the love of God and your absolute fulfilment in him.

(135) The third stage is that of inner certainty which banishes all fear. You're so intoxicated with God's love at this stage and so resigned to his will, that, if it were his wish, you would willingly go to hell for him. It's at this point that you most definitely experience the powerful bond of divine union, which makes it seem impossible for you to be

separated from your beloved God and his boundless treasure.

(136) There are another six stages of contemplation, which are: fire, unction, exaltation, enlightenment, pleasure, and rest. At the first stage, that of fire, the soul is alight, and being alight, is anointed, and being anointed is exalted, and exalted it contemplates, and in taking pleasure it rests and reposes. By these stages the soul that is experienced and abstracted from all particularities ascends on the interior and spiritual way.

(137) At the first stage, which is that of fire, the soul is illumined by a burning ray of divine light that kindles affection and dries up emotion that is merely human. The second stage is that of unction, which is a gentle and spiritual effulgence that is diffused in the soul and that informs it, strengthens it, and disposes it to receive and contemplate the divine truth. Sometimes this divine effulgence extends as far as human nature itself, thereby increasing its capacity for tolerance, and imparting pleasurable sensations with intimations of eternity.

(138) The third stage is that of the exaltation of interior persons to a state that transcends the limitations of self, to a realm where they may drink more fully from the clear fountain of pure love.

(139) The fourth stage, which is that of enlightenment, is an infused knowledge that emanates from the divine truth, which is soft and gentle, and where the soul delights in contemplation thereby acquiring ever greater clarity and light, for it is led by the divine spirit itself.

(140) The fifth stage is an exquisite appreciation of the divine gentleness that streams out from the plentiful and fecund spring of the Holy Spirit.

(141) The sixth is a tender and consummate tranquillity that is born of the victory over interior conflict and the practice of frequent prayer, an experience vouchsafed to few, if any. At this point joy and peace are of such magnitude that the soul seems to be softly asleep and enjoys complete solace and serenity while at rest on the divine and loving breast.

(142) There are many other stages in contemplation such as ecstasies, raptures, jubilation, exultation, union, transformation, spiritual betrothal and marriage, which I omit to explain here to avoid speculation, and because there are entire books given over to these matters, although all these states are like colour to a blind person, or harmony to a deaf one, if they're not experienced at first hand. In short, we ascend by these stages to the dwelling place of the king of all serenity, and to the true wisdom of Solomon.

Chapter 16

Signs by which to know interior persons and purified souls

(143) There are four signs by which to know interior persons. First, the understanding produces no other thoughts than those that encourage the light of faith, and the disciplined will produces no other acts of love than those directed to God, and which pertain to God. Second, when persons cease from any outward activity in which they may be engaged, then their understanding and will turn back to God with ease. Third, on entering prayer all things are forgotten, as if they had never existed. And last, they behave toward outward affairs as though they were seeing them afresh, but at the same time they will be wary of involving themselves in worldly concerns, having a natural aversion to them, unless charity requires their involvement in them.

(144) Such persons are now free in their dealings with exterior concerns and find it easy to enter their interior solitude, where they see only God, and themselves in God, and where they adore God with quietness, peace and true love, for in this their most intimate centre God tenderly communes with them, revealing to them a new kingdom, true joy, and peace.

(145) The interior peace of spiritual, abstracted, and inwardly-focused persons remains inviolate, even though they suffer outward conflict, because storms cannot reach across the vast distances to that most serene interior haven, where pure and perfect love dwells, for although at times they find themselves defenceless and isolated they know that it's only on the outside that the storm rages.

(146) This intimate love produces four effects. The first is enlightenment, which is a peerless empirical knowledge of the grandeur of God and of your own nothingness. The second effect may be likened to a soul that's alight with a burning desire to be consumed, like the salamander in the tenderness of the divine fire. The third is tenderness itself, which is a state of serene, joyous, gentle and intimate fulfilment. The fourth is an absorption of all your faculties in God, for by this time your powers are so enraptured and intoxicated in God that the soul is incapable of seeking, desiring or wanting anything other than the Highest Good.

(147) From this complete satiety come two effects. The first is a tremendous courage to suffer for God. The second is a certain hope or assurance that you will never lose God or be separated from him. Those who aspire to perfection discipline their passions; having done this, they deny themselves; then, with divine assistance, they enter the Void, where the ego has no place, self-will is set at naught, and they reach a state of awareness where they realize that of themselves they are nothing, that they can do nothing, and that they are worth nothing. From this position they die to senses and self, in many ways and at all times; and finally, from this spiritual death arises true and perfect annihilation. And so, when you're dead to your desires and understanding you may justifiably be said to have arrived at a perfect state of joyous annihilation without any awareness on your part, for you would not be annihilated if you were conscious of the fact. And although you've attained this happy state of annihilation, it's important to remember that you've yet more distance to travel, more to purify, and more to annihilate.

(148) According to St Thomas Aquinas, the purified soul is known by three signs. The first is diligence, which is the strength of spirit that banishes all negligence and idleness and disposes you to practise virtue earnestly and confidently. The second is severity, which is strength of spirit against lust and is accompanied by a keen love of asperity, an appropriate awareness of your own insignificance, and poverty of spirit. The third is kindliness, which is a gentleness of spirit that banishes all rancour, envy, and hatred of, and aversion to, other people.

(149) Until your spirit is purged, your emotions purified, your memory stripped, your understanding enlightened, your will denied and set on fire, you will never attain intimate and loving union with God, for as the spirit of God is light, tranquillity, and purity itself, so too must you cherish purity, peace, tranquillity, and be absolutely focused on God. In brief, the precious gift of the purified spirit belongs to those who assiduously cultivate love and who consider their own egos to be of no significance whatsoever.

Chapter 17

On divine wisdom

(150) Divine wisdom is an infused and intuitive understanding of divine perfection and of things eternal, and should be called contemplation rather than speculation. Science is acquired knowledge and provides an understanding of nature. Wisdom is received passively and provides an understanding of divine goodness. The former pursues knowledge by dint of hard work and effort; the latter prefers to be unknowing about what it knows, although in fact such knowledge is the highest attainment. In a word, scientists are limited to knowledge about material matters while the truly wise live immersed in God.

(151) The trained mind of the wise demonstrates a superior and heightened spiritual awareness, which provides them with acute insight into whatever is unworthy of them in relation to their life and position. Wisdom is what makes such people natural, percipient, balanced, spiritual, completely focused on God, and abstracted from all material things. This state is what moves and impels those meek and lowly of heart to gentle but energetic action by filling them with peace and kindliness. In brief, we recall what the wise man said on this matter: "But with this wisdom there came to me all good things together" (Wis. 7:11).

(152) Most people live according to their own lights and form judgments based on the fallibility of their senses and reasoning powers. But the wise judge everything according to its intrinsic merit, the effects of which are genuine understanding, insight, and the ability to penetrate the meaning of, and transcend, all created existence, including the ego.

(153) It's very characteristic of the wise to do much and to say little.

(154) Wisdom shows itself in the words and deeds of the wise, because as they're master of all their passions, activities and emotions, this quality is evident in their daily life, and is like still, quiet water in which wisdom can be seen to shine with great clarity.

(155) The understanding of the true mystic is hidden and inaccessible to those who are purely scholastic because it's an

understanding which, although common to saints, is not readily available except to those who are committed to the love of others and to the suppression of their own ego. But those who do commit themselves to this life become purely mystical and possessed of true humility, which enables them to acquire a profound awareness of the Divinity, whereas the more people emphasize the sensual life of flesh and blood, the more they distance themselves from mystical knowledge.

(156) Ordinarily, in those who have great scholastic and speculative knowledge, divine wisdom is not a dominant feature, but when you have the two together they make an admirable combination. For this reason the learned doctors of the Church, who by the grace of God became mystics, are worthy of veneration and praise.

(157) Mystics and the wise carry out their activities passively rather than actively, and though these may bring them intense suffering, nevertheless they perform them prudently and meticulously.

(158) The sermons of learned people who aren't imbued with the spirit, though consisting of ingenious stories, elegant descriptions, clever reasoning and sophisticated texts, are in no way the word of God, but the word of men, and for this reason are adulterated gold. These preachers corrupt other Christians by filling them with empty rhetoric and so both remain empty of God. Teachers like these feed their flocks with poisonous subtleties, giving them stones for bread, leaves for fruit, and instead of genuine nourishment, tasteless food mixed with poisonous honey. These people are status-seekers who set great store by their own reputation and esteem instead of seeking the glory of God and the spiritual edification of those who depend on them.

(159) Those who preach earnestly and sincerely preach for God; those who preach otherwise preach for themselves. Those who preach the word of God from the heart impress it on the hearts of others; the words of those who don't preach from the heart reach only as far as the ear. Perfection doesn't consist in teaching, but in doing, for those who know a lot of truths aren't holier and wiser unless they put these truths into practice.

(160) It's self-evident that divine wisdom produces humility and the knowledge acquired by the learned leads merely to pride.

(161) Sanctity doesn't consist of the ability to form lofty and subtle concepts regarding the knowledge and attributes of God, but in love for God and the denial of self-will. It's for this reason that sanctity is found more usually in the sincere and humble than in the learned. How often will you find little old ladies without erudition but rich in the love of God! And how often you find conceited theologians full of empty learning and totally bereft of genuine light and charity!

(162) You will be well advised to bear in mind that you should

always talk as one willing to learn rather than as one who knows it all, and to prefer people to think of you as lacking in learning rather than as someone who is wise and knowledgeable.

(163) Although those versed in purely speculative knowledge will understand through study some small spark of the spirit, this doesn't derive from the pure depths of divine wisdom, which has a mortal hatred of concepts and ideas, for discursive thinking is always an obstacle to eternal, profound, pure, sincere, and genuine wisdom.

Chapter 18

Continuation

(164) There are two ways that lead to a knowledge of God: one is indirect, the other direct. The first way is called speculation and the second contemplation. The learned who follow the way of scientific speculation with its emphasis on the use of reason seek God by this means as best they can, hoping that in this they may be helped to a love of God. Yet no one who follows this scholastic way will arrive by it alone to the mystical way or to the excellence of union, transformation, simplicity, light, peace, tranquillity, and love, unlike those who are led by divine grace along the mystical way of contemplation.

(165) Those people who are merely scholastic don't know what the spirit is, and neither do they know what it is to lose themselves in God, or experience intense joy in their most innermost being where God has his throne and communicates himself with indescribable and exquisite warmth. On the contrary, some of them are incapable of grasping this knowledge at all (because no one can understand without having experienced it), and therefore they condemn it, and moreover they're feted and applauded for their opinions, and this because of the lack of light in the world and an excess of ignorance.

(166) The reason that theologians don't enjoy the gentleness of contemplation is that they don't enter by the gate St Paul mentions when he says: "If any man thinks that he is wise among you in this world, let him become a fool that he may become wise" (1 Cor. 3:18). And so, if there are those among you who consider yourselves wise, be a fool, and so attain wisdom, and be humble and have others think that you're ignorant.

(167) As a general rule, indeed as a truism, practice must precede theory in mystical theology. There should first be some experience in the practice of supernatural contemplation before you look into it and investigate the phenomenon.

(168) Although mystical knowledge is more usually associated with the humble and the innocent, this doesn't necessarily mean that the

learned are incapable of acquiring it, so long as they don't pander to their own egos, or rely on the shortcomings of the erudition they've managed to achieve by themselves. They really have more of a chance of gaining mystical knowledge if they forget about their own learning and disregard it, and make use of it only at the appropriate time and place in preaching and discussion, and afterwards devote themselves entirely to the simple, naked contemplation of God, which is devoid of any conceptual form or feature.

(169) Study that's not intended solely for the glory of God is a short road to perdition – not because of the study itself, but for the empty pride to which it gives rise. Most people these days are deficient in this way, as they study only to satisfy the insatiable curiosity of human nature.

(170) Many people seek God but don't find him because they're driven more by curiosity than by a sincere and single-minded intent; they would rather have spiritual consolation than God himself, and because they don't seek him in truth, they find neither God nor spiritual consolation.

(171) Those who aren't trying totally to deny themselves will never be really detached and so can never receive the truth and the light of the spirit.

(172) Those who place a higher value on listening than talking are very rare. Wise and truly mystical people don't speak unless they have to, or meddle in what doesn't concern them, and if they have to become involved, then they do so only cautiously.

(173) The spirit of divine wisdom fills you with kindliness, informs with firmness, and is a perfect guide to those who accept its discipline.

(174) Those endowed with divine wisdom appreciate all things for their innate goodness and not merely for their appearance.

(175) Where the divine spirit dwells you will always find simplicity and freedom, whereas cunning, duplicity, deceit, slyness, and unhealthy interest in political machinations are anathema to the wise and sincere.

(176) To acquire mystical knowledge you must avoid and become detached from five things. First, the created world; second, worldly concerns; third, the gifts of the Holy Spirit themselves; fourth, yourself; and fifth, God himself. This last detachment is the most important of all, for those who can do this succeed in losing themselves in God, and only those who lose themselves can be sure of finding themselves.

(177) God appreciates your capacity for affection more than your knowledge of worldly matters. It's one thing to purify your heart of everything that imprisons and defiles it, and quite another to do a hundred and one good deeds, however laudable, if by the same token you don't attend to the purity of your heart, which is the chief means of acquiring divine wisdom.

(178) There are many people who fail to attain quiet contemplation, divine wisdom, and genuine knowledge, even though they spend many hours in prayer and take communion every day, because they don't surrender themselves to God with perfect nakedness and detachment. Finally, until you're purified in the fire of inward and outward torment you will never attain to the state of renewal, transformation, perfect contemplation, loving union, and divine wisdom.

Chapter 19

On true and perfect annihilation

(179) The workshop of annihilation is founded on just two principles. The first is to have a low regard for your own importance and for all temporal things, from which attitude should come a willingness to put into practice complete abnegation of yourself and everything else, and this in a very whole-hearted, energetic and determined manner.

(180) The second principle is to hold God in the highest esteem, by loving him, adoring him, and following him without the least self-interest, however well-intentioned this may be. From the practice of these two principles utter conformity to the divine will emerges. This powerful and practical conformity to God in all things leads to annihilation and transformation in God with no admixture of raptures, ecstasies, or excessive intensity of emotion. You must bear in mind that this road is fraught with many illusions and carries with it the danger of illness and mental exhaustion, and if you take this turning you will be very unlikely to reach the peak of perfection, for this is attained by the other genuine, safe and reliable path, though not without a heavy cross to bear, which is the royal road to annihilation and perfection. If you follow this road you will be the recipient of many divine gifts of light and love, yet the annihilated must detach themselves even from these gifts if they're not to be an impediment to their eventual deification.

(181) At the same time as you eschew the gratification of the ego you must follow the road of annihilation, which consists in disdain for the pursuit of honour, dignity and acclaim, for there's no reason to undermine your progress in self-denial and humility by flattering the ego with a dignity and honour that inflate your sense of importance.

(182) It seems impossible to those without an inflated sense of their own worth that they could be deserving of anything – on the contrary, they're more likely to be embarrassed and assert their unworthiness of any claim to fame and virtue. Such people bear with equanimity all those occasions they're insulted, harassed, held in contempt, and affronted, for they believe they're deserving of such

opprobrium. In fact, they give thanks to God when they find themselves in these situations, as they feel they're no less than they deserve, and even feel unworthy that God sees fit to test them in this way. Above all, they are glad of the opportunity to tolerate contempt and insult as they feel this is to God's greater glory.

(183) Additionally, such people always accord themselves the lowest possible status, both as regards to their position and style of dress and everything else, without having any pretensions to uniqueness. They believe that the lowest of positions is more than they deserve, and that they're unworthy even of this. And so if they continue with this attitude they will attain to genuine self-annihilation.

(184)Those who aspire to perfection discipline their passions; having done this, they deny themselves; then, with divine assistance, they enter the Void, where the ego has no place, self-will is set at naught, and they reach a state of awareness where they realize that of themselves they are nothing, that they can do nothing, and that they are worth nothing. From this position they die to senses and self, in many ways and at all times; and finally, from this spiritual death arises true and perfect annihilation. And so, when you're dead to your desires and understanding you may justifiably be said to have arrived at a perfect state of joyous annihilation without any awareness on your part, for you would not be annihilated if you were conscious of the fact. And although you've attained this happy state of annihilation, it's important to remember that you've yet more distance to travel, more to purify, and more to annihilate.

(185) For this annihilation to be perfect it must obliterate your own judgment, will, emotions, inclinations, desires, thoughts, and the ego itself. And so finally, you must be dead to wanting, desiring, striving, understanding and thinking: wanting as if you were not wanting, desiring as if not desiring, understanding as if not understanding, thinking as if not thinking, devoid of all inclination, and accepting contempt in the same spirit as honour, and advantage in the same way as punishment.

(186) Oh, how blessed are those who are dead and annihilated in this way! For now they live not for themselves, but God lives in them. And in all truth we can say that they're like the phoenix, because they're reborn, changed, spiritualized, transformed, and deified.

Chapter 20

How the void is the short cut to attain purity of spirit, perfect contemplation and the rich treasure of interior peace

(187) The means to arrive at this exalted state of renewal, and the most immediate way to be united to the Highest Good, to your primordial origin and supreme peace, is the Void. Endeavour always to be immersed in this Void of your nothingness, for it's God's way of working miracles in your soul. Clothe yourself in this Void and strive for it to be your constant support and dwelling place, until you lose yourself in it, and I assure you that if you're always in the Void, then God will be fully in your soul.

(188) Why do you think that there are so many who obstruct this abundant flow of God's gifts? Because they want to interfere and feel important, never reminding themselves of their insignificance and nothingness, and so denying the miracles that God wants to work in them. And so long as they're attached to the gifts of the spirit in themselves, which leads them to desert the core of the Void, then they spoil everything. They don't truly seek God, and so they don't find him. You must realize that God is found only when we're unmindful of ourselves and when we remain in the Void.

(189) We seek only ourselves whenever we emerge from this Void, and therefore we never arrive at a quiet, perfect contemplation. Enter within the reality of your own nothingness and nothing will make you anxious: humble yourself, and forget your own self-importance.

(190) What strength you will find in this Void! Who will trouble you if you take refuge in this fortress? Those who think little of themselves, and who don't give themselves airs, can be hurt by nobody, and those who rest in the Void know interior silence and live transformed in the Highest Good. They require nothing from this world, and live immersed in God, resigned in all suffering, because they feel that this is the least they should expect. When your soul is silent in the Void, the Lord perfects it, enriches it and impresses upon it his own image and likeness.

(191) You must strive to lose yourself in God through the Void, which is your supreme perfection, and if you succeed in losing yourself you will be content, you will gain power over yourself, and you will be sure to find yourself. In this workshop of the Void sincerity of spirit is wrought, and interior and infused contemplation is received, serenity is assured, and your heart purified from all manner of imperfection. What a treasure you will find if you make your dwelling-place in this Void! And if you penetrate to its core you will not meddle in extraneous matters (the stumbling block for so many) and involve yourself only in those affairs that concern you.

(192) If you're enclosed in your nothingness, where the blows of adversity cannot reach you, nothing will harm you, nothing will make you anxious. It's here that you gain mastery of yourself, for only here reigns true and perfect power. With this shield of the Void you will overcome the strongest temptation and the direst provocations of the jealous enemy.

(193) Knowing that you're nothing, that you can do nothing, and that you yourself are nothing, you will calmly endure the passive aridities, you will tolerate the most awful bleakness of spirit, and you will suffer spiritual and interior torment. By means of the Void you will die to yourself in many ways, at all times, and at all hours. And the more you die to yourself, the less will you consider your own importance, and the more God will increase you and unite you with him.

(194) Who will awaken your soul from this sweet and delightful sleep, if you rest in the Void? When you're immersed in this emptiness, you close the door to everything that's not God; you will give up your own self-love and you will journey to that interior solitude where the Divine Bridegroom speaks to the heart of his bride, revealing to her the most exalted wisdom. Sink into this Void and you will find a sacred refuge in all adversity.

(195) And so in this way you will return to that joyful state of innocence that our first parents lost. By this door you will enter the joyous land of the living, where you will find the Highest Good, the full breadth of charity, the beauty of justice, the straight line of fairness and integrity: in short, total perfection. Finally, think nothing, desire nothing, want nothing, know nothing, and your soul will dwell in serenity and joy in all things. This is the way to purity of spirit, perfect contemplation, and interior peace. Journey without ceasing along this safe path, and endeavour to submerge yourself in the Void and to lose yourself in it if you're truly to annihilate yourself, to become one with God, and to be transformed.

Chapter 21

On the supreme happiness of interior peace, and its wonderful effects

(196) Being now annihilated and reborn in perfect nakedness of spirit you will experience a profound peace and delightful quiet in the superior part of your soul, which leads you to such a perfect loving union that you exult in all things. You're possessed of such joy that your only desire is to do your beloved's bidding, and in so doing you will accept all events with equal equanimity, be they pleasurable or distressing, for your overriding concern is to act in complete accordance with the divine will.

(197) At this stage there's nothing that displeases you and nothing that afflicts you; to die is joy, and to live is bliss. You're as happy on earth as you would be in paradise, as content in privation as with possession, as glad in sickness as in health, for you accept everything as God's will. This is your life, your glory, your paradise, your peace, your serenity, your tranquillity, your complete comfort and consolation, and your supreme happiness.

(198) If, having ascended by the steps of annihilation to the realm of peace, we were faced with a choice, we would choose desolation rather than consolation, disdain before honour, because our loving Jesus himself set great store by our ability to bear suffering and opprobrium. If at first we hungered for heaven's blessings, if we thirsted after God and feared to lose him, if we suffered sorrow in our heart and endured the struggle against evil, then now our hunger will be satisfied, our thirst will be assuaged, our fear will give way to assurance, our sadness will turn to joy, and the ferocious struggle will be replaced by supreme peace. Happy are those who enjoy such bliss on earth! These people, though few in number, are the stout columns that support the Church and mitigate the divine wrath.

(199) Those who have entered this heavenly peace are replete with God and his supernatural gifts because they live grounded in pure love and are equally at home in light as in darkness, in night as in day, and in affliction as in consolation. With this holy and heavenly indifference they never lose their peace in adversity, or their tranquillity in tribulation, but on the contrary are filled with ineffable joy.

(200) Although the prince of darkness mounts all the assaults of hell against them by means of awful temptation, they resist like a strong pillar, and may be compared in this way to the high mountain and the deep valley during a storm.

(201) The valley is darkened with thick cloud and endures fierce hail storms, thunder, and bolts of lightning, so that it resembles a picture of hell, while at the same time the high mountain is resplendent, bathed in beautiful sunlight in peace and tranquillity, all of it shining like a clear sky, bright and pacific.

(202) The same thing happens to these fortunate persons. The valley of their inferior nature suffers distress, conflict, darkness, desolation, torment, anguish and temptations. At the same time, on the high mountain of their superior nature, the sun casts its light and inflames and illumines them, so that they remain clear, peaceful, resplendent, tranquil and serene, and transformed into an ocean of joy.

(203) Such is the quiet of pure souls that have reached the peak of the mountain of tranquillity, such is the peace in their spirit, and such their interior serenity that there radiates outward also a trace and glimmer of God.

(204) On this throne of tranquillity the perfection of spiritual beauty is made manifest, for here is the true light of the secrets and mysteries of our holy faith; perfect humility and self-annihilation; complete resignation, purity, poverty of spirit, the innocence and simplicity of a dove, outward modesty, inward silence and solitude, freedom and purity of heart; obliviousness of the created world, and of oneself; joyful simplicity, heavenly indifference, continuous prayer, total nakedness, perfect detachment, the highest knowledge of contemplation, communion with heaven, and finally, the most perfect and serene interior peace, allowing us to say of the joyous soul that has attained this perfection what the wise man said of wisdom, namely, that all the other graces come with it: "But with her came to me all good things together" (Wis. 7:11).

(205) This is the rich and hidden treasure. This is the lost drachma of the Gospel. This is the life of the blessed, the only true life, and bliss on earth. Oh, magnificent grandeur that transcends the understanding of the children of men! How exquisite is the supernal life, how wonderful, how ineffable, how utterly blissful! How exalted is the soul that has lost sight of all the earth's depravity! Although it is outwardly poor, inwardly it is full of wealth; it appears lowly, but it is exalted. In short, it is now possible for us to live the divine life here on earth. I beseech you, God of all goodness, to allow me this celestial bliss and the true peace that this world, enslaved by its senses, is incapable of understanding or receiving.

Chapter 22

A heartfelt plea and lament to God that so few people attain perfection, loving union, and divine transformation

(206) Oh, divine majesty, in whose presence the pillars of heaven do quake and tremble! Oh, infinite goodness in whose love the seraphim burn! Allow me, oh my Lord, to grieve for our blindness and ingratitude. All of us live a lie, placing our trust in a foolish world, forsaking you, our God. All of us reject you, the fountain of living waters, for the fetid waters of this world.

(207) Oh, children of men! For how long shall we go on seeking refuge in lies and emptiness? Who is it that deceives us, that leads us astray from our God, the Highest Good? And who is it that speaks to us the greatest truth, that loves us most, that defends us best? Where will we find a finer friend, a more tender bridegroom, a better father? Oh, that our blindness should be so pervasive that we should all want to forgo this supreme goodness!

(208) Oh heavenly Father, how few there are who serve you perfectly! Who are those willing to suffer, to follow Christ crucified, to embrace the Cross and to deny themselves? Oh, how few there are who achieve detachment and total nakedness of spirit, who die to themselves and are alive to God, and who totally resign themselves to his divine will! How few there are who live a life of simple obedience with profound self-knowledge and true humility, who surrender themselves into God's hands with absolute indifference to themselves that he may do with them as he wishes! How few there are who are detached and pure in heart, devoid of understanding, knowledge, wanting and desiring, and who yearn for annihilation and spiritual death! How few there are who allow the heavenly creator to work within them, who suffer by not suffering, and die by not dying, who are willing to forget themselves and strip their heart of emotions, desires, satisfactions, self-love and their own judgment! Who are those that allow themselves to be led along the royal road of negation and

the interior way, who are willing to be annihilated by dying to themselves and their senses, who are prepared to be emptied, purified and stripped that God may clothe them, fill them and perfect them? Finally, oh Lord, how few there are who are truly contemplative and blind, deaf and dumb to the world of the senses!

(209) Oh, the shame of the children of Adam, who out of depravity despise true joy, who renounce the Highest Good and lose this rich treasure and infinite goodness! With good reason does heaven lament that there are so few who are willing to follow its wonderful ways: "The ways of Zion do mourn, for none come to this solemn assembly" (Lam. 1:4).